# MANAGING PEOPLE
## IS LIKE

Herding Cats

# WARREN BENNIS

ON LEADERSHIP

For permissions requests, contact the publisher at:

Executive Excellence Publishing
1344 East 1120 South
Provo, UT 84606
phone: (801) 375-4060
fax: (801) 377-5960
www.eep.com

Printed in the United States of America
2nd Printing, 2000

ISBN 1-890009-61-X
Also available on audio, ISBN: 1-890009-10-5

Cover design by Heather Stratford-Innes
Cover illustration by Gabe Bonilla
Printed by Publishers Press

*For Grace*

# CONTENTS

# PREFACE

# CATS AND RATS

During my term as a university president, I always felt that presiding over the faculty was like herding cats. And my saying about faculty members is that "if you meet one, you meet one."

But such individualism is part of what makes leading a group of knowledge workers so exciting, and so challenging.

Increasingly, in the United States and throughout the world, leaders must respect individual rights, tastes, opinions, and idiosyncrasies. Whether their organizations are funded by taxes or tithing, endowments or product sales, wise leaders know that the proverbial "widow's mite" is what makes their exalted positions possible. Each widow, therefore, commands respect.

Anymore, managing any people is like herding cats. Cats, of course, won't allow themselves to be herded. They may, however, be coaxed, cajoled, persuaded, adored, and gently led. With cats, keep in mind, the dictum is milk before meat. Any leader who dares to think of himself or herself as the "cat's meow" will likely be hissed and clawed. The recipe calls for more catnip, less catnap.

In his *Old Possum's Book of Practical Cats*, T. S. Eliot writes of The Rum Tum Tugger, "For he will do as he will do, and there's no doing anything about it. When you let him in, then he wants to be out; he's always on the wrong side of every door."

Gone are the days when leaders and managers—even dictators and despots—could afford to think of people in terms of gangs and groups, databases and demographics, masses and markets, cultures and castes.

Indeed, from Delphi to Shanghai, the oracles now bow to common individuals. There is no leadership Shangri-la. Even in Bali and Tahiti, government and business leaders must now suit up when meeting with constituents. In classrooms, administrators and teachers can't just shout, "Sit down, shut up, and listen." Students expect interaction. In Cuba and Iran, dictators Fidel Castro and Saddam Hussein have to listen to voices of individual dissidents to maintain power.

Why? Because today people have options and opinions; they have money and mobility; they have education and experience; they have personal computers, modems, faxes, e-mail, CD-ROM and the Internet. In sum, they have information. What was once, not many months ago, stored only in management's heads and files, is now on everyone's computer. And the first consequence of the so-called "open office" is the oft-banned "open mind."

When I started my studies of leadership about 15 years ago, I consulted with a lot of people, including an old friend, who still teaches at the Harvard Business School. I told him I wanted to go out and spend the next 10 or 20 years seeing if I could identify the basic characteristics of exemplary, outstanding, excellent leaders to see what they were made up of, what their character was like.

My friend sort of scoffed at me and said, "Look, the only thing we can ever say about leadership is that it's like pornography. You can't describe it; you can't define it, but you know it when you see it." He said, "I think it's arrogant of you to think you're going to go out and do that." When he used the word "arrogant" to describe me, I reminded him of the Harvard University professor's prayer "Dear Lord, please deliver us from the terrible sin of intellectual arrogance, which for your information means . . ."

So, to you who aspire to lead people, I again say: Be humble. Stop trying to "herd cats" and start building trust and mutual respect. Your "cats" will respond. They will sense your purpose, keep your business purring, and even kill your rats.

Warren Bennis

# INTRODUCTION

# AN INVENTED LIFE

*We all face the great challenge to discover our native abilities
and to invent and reinvent ourselves throughout life.*

I believe in self-invention as an exercise of the imagination. That's basically how we get to know ourselves. People who can't invent and reinvent themselves must be content with borrowed postures, secondhand ideas, fitting in instead of standing out. Inventing oneself is the opposite of accepting the roles we were brought up to play.

To be authentic is literally to be your own author (the words are derived from the same Greek root), to discover your native energies and desires, and then to find your own way of acting on them. When you've done that, you are not existing simply to live up to an image posited by the culture, family tradition, or some other authority. When you write your own life, you play the game that is natural for you to play. You keep covenant with your own promise.

## My Own Roots

The landscape of my childhood was very like a Beckett stage set—barren, meager, endless. A little boy waited there for someone who might not, probably would not, show up. There were walk-ons occasionally: twin brothers 10 years my senior, a father who worked eighteen hours a day (when he took off his shoes and soiled socks, the ring of dirt around his ankles had to be scrubbed off with a stiff-bristled brush), and a mother who liked vaudeville and played mah-jongg with her friends when she wasn't helping my father eke out an existence.

I was withdrawn, sullen, detached, removed from hope or desire, and probably depressed—"mopey," my father called it. I was also left pretty much alone. I had no close friends. I can't remember how I spent my time, except I know that I made up improved versions of my life that ran like 24-hour newsreels in my mind.

I didn't much like school, and barely remember most of my teachers, except for Miss Shirer. I liked Miss Shirer enormously. She taught the eighth grade, and she was almost famous because her older brother, William Shirer, was broadcasting from Berlin on CBS. I leaned into the radio whenever Shirer was on. That he was anti-Hitler was thrilling to a kid who, in 1938, often felt like the only Jew in Westwood, New Jersey, a town that richly deserved its reputation as a major stronghold of the German Bund.

On one momentous occasion, Miss Shirer asked us to spend about ten minutes telling the class about our favorite hobby. I panicked. After all, I liked Miss Shirer a lot, but the truth was that I didn't have anything remotely like a favorite hobby. My efforts to develop recreational interests like those of the other guys had failed miserably. I was mediocre at sports. I was bored with stamps. I was too clumsy to tie dry flies, too nervous to hunt, too maladroit to build model airplanes out of balsa wood. What I finally decided to do, in a moment of desperate inspiration, was to bring a shoebox full of shoe polish—different colors and shades in cans and bottles—since the only palpable physical activity I regularly engaged in was shining the family shoes.

And so when it was my turn in the spotlight, I revealed the arcane nature of a new art form. I described in loving detail the nuances of my palette (I was especially good on the subtle differences between oxblood and maroon). I discoursed on the form and function of the various appliances needed to achieve an impressive tone and sheen. I argued both sides of the debate on solid versus liquid wax and wrapped it all up with a spirited disquisition on the multiple virtues of Neat's foot oil. It was a remarkable performance, if only because it was, from start to finish, an act of pure imagination. I could tell from her smile that Miss Shirer thought it was terrific. Even the class seemed impressed in a stupefied way. And there, in a flourish of brushes and shoe polish, a new Warren Bennis was born.

### Army and School

When I graduated from high school into the army during World War II (1943 to 1947), I saw firsthand the consequences of good and bad leadership in the simplest and starkest terms—morale, tank support that would or would not be where it was supposed to be, wounds, body counts. The army was the first organization I was to observe close-up and in-depth. And although I have been in more pleasant classrooms, it was an excellent place to study such organizational realities as the effects of command-and-control leadership and the paralyzing impact of institutional bureaucracy. The army also taught me the value of being organized.

Once out of the army, I attended Antioch College (1947 to 1951), where I learned to have opinions. That may not sound very important, but it amounted to a personal paradigm shift. What freedom, what liberation, to have opinions. Having opinions was, at least for me, tantamount to developing a personal identity.

To get through the Ph.D. program at MIT (1951 to 1956), I began to memorize and mimic. I imitated my professors and the brightest of my fellow graduate students. For roughly two years, I lip-synced what I heard, Milli Vanilli style. Eventually, the words I formed on my lips came more naturally, but I often wondered whether I was kidding myself.

From 1955 to 1971, I made stops in Bethel, Maine, where everyone was buzzing over Kurt Lewin's T-groups; Boston University, where I taught psychology and underwent psychoanalysis; and SUNY Buffalo, where I learned that unless a vision is sustained by action, it quickly turns to ashes.

President Martin Meyerson's bold dream never got out of the administration building. In ways that only later became clear, we undermined the very thing we wanted most. Our actions and even our style tended to alienate the people who would be most affected by the changes we proposed. Failing to appreciate the importance to the organization of the people who are already in it is a classic managerial mistake, one that new managers and change-oriented administrators are especially prone to make. We certainly did. In our Porsches and berets, we acted as if the organization hadn't existed until the day we arrived.

There are no clean slates in established organizations. A new administration can't play Noah and build the world anew with two handpicked representatives of each academic discipline. Talk of new beginnings is so much rhetoric—frightening rhetoric to those who suspect that the new signals the end of their own careers. At Buffalo we newcomers disregarded history. But without history, without continuity, there can be no success-ful change. Alfred North Whitehead said it best: "Every leader, to be effective, must simultaneously adhere to the symbols of change and revision and the symbols of tradition and stability."

What most of us in organizations really want (and what sta-tus, money, and power serve as currency for) is acceptance, affection, self-esteem. Institutions are more amenable to change when the esteem of all members is preserved and enhanced. Whatever people say, given economic sufficiency, they stay in organizations and feel satisfied in them because they feel com-petent and valued. Change carries the threat of loss. When managers remove that threat, people are much freer to identify with the adaptive process and much better equipped to tolerate the high degree of ambiguity that accompanies change.

When I think of Buffalo, I think of that joke "How many psychiatrists does it take to change a light bulb?" The answer is "One, but the light bulb really has to want to change." Organizations change themselves when the members want to. You can't force them to change, even in a Batman cape.

### University President

As president of the University of Cincinnati (1971 to 1978), I finally realized that my principal role model was going to have to be me. I decided that the kind of university president I want-ed to be was one who led, not managed. That's an important difference. Many an institution is well-managed yet very poor-ly led. It excels in the ability to handle all the daily routine inputs yet never asks whether the routine should be done in the first place.

My entrapment in minutiae made me realize another thing: that people were following the old army game. They did not want to take responsibility for the decisions they properly should make. "Let's push up the tough ones" had become the motto. As a result, everybody was dumping his or her "wet babies" (as old hands at the State Department call them) on my desk. I decided then and there that my highest priority was to create an "executive constellation" to run the office of the president. The sole requirements for inclusion in the group were that the individual needed to know more than I did about his or her area of competence and had to be willing to take care of daily matters without referring them back to me. I was going to make the time to lead.

I realized that I had been doing what so many leaders do: I was trying to be everything to the organization—father, fixer, policeman, ombudsman, rabbi, therapist, and banker. As a CEO who was similarly afflicted put it to me later, "If I'm walking on the shop floor and see a leak in the dike, I have to stick my finger in." Trying to be everything to everyone was diverting me from real leadership. It was burning me out. And perhaps worst of all, it was denying all the potential leaders under me the chance to learn and prove themselves.

Things got better after that, although I never came close to the ideal. As I look back at my experience at UC, I compare it with my psychoanalysis: I wouldn't have missed it for the world, and I would never go through it again. In becoming a leader I learned a number of important things about both leadership and myself. As Sophocles observes in *Antigone*, "But hard it is to learn the mind of any mortal, or the heart, 'til he be tried in chief authority. Power shows the man."

Having executive power showed me some personal truths. First, I was, as the song says, "looking for love in all the wrong places." Intellectually I knew that leaders can't, shouldn't, count on being loved. But I seriously underestimated the emotional impact of angry constituents. I believed the false dream that people would love me if only they really got to know me. I call it the Lennie Bernstein syndrome. Ned Rorem, Leonard Bernstein's friend and colleague, recalls how "Lennie" was furious about a negative review in the *New York Times*. "That critic hates me," Bernstein said. Rorem suggested gently that Bernstein really couldn't expect everyone to love him. Bernstein was stunned for a moment by his friend's insight. "Oh, yeah," Bernstein finally conceded, "that's because you can't meet everybody."

Anyone in authority, astronaut or baseball player, university president or national leader, is to some extent the hostage of how others perceive him or her. The perceptions of other people can be a prison. For the first time I began to understand what it must be like to be the victim of prejudice, to be helpless in the steel embrace of how other people see you. People impute motives to their leaders, love or hate them, seek them out or avoid them, and idolize or demonize them independently of what leaders do or are. Ironically, at the very time I had the most power, I felt the greatest sense of powerlessness.

And I realized an important personal truth. I was never going to be completely happy with positional power, the only kind of power an organization can bestow. What I really wanted was personal power, influence based on voice.

### Autumn of My Days

I am now in my seventeenth year at the University of Southern California—my longest continuous tenure at any institution. In many ways it has been the happiest period of my life. USC has provided me with exactly the right social architecture to do what seems most important to me now: teaching in the broadest sense.

At USC I have the leisure to consolidate what I've learned about self-invention, about the importance of organization, about the nature of change, about the nature of leadership— and to find ways to communicate those lessons. Erik Erikson talks about an eight-stage process of human development. I think I have entered Erikson's seventh stage—the generative one—in which self-absorption gives way to an altruistic surrender to the next generation. Although writing is my greatest joy, I also take enormous pleasure in people-growing, in watching others bloom, in mentoring as I was mentored.

What I have already discovered is that the need to reinvent oneself, to "compose a life," as Mary Catherine Bateson puts it, is ongoing. Some years ago, I took a summer course on Dickens at Trinity Hall, Cambridge, with my closest friend, Sam Jaffe, who was then 89. Sam, who in his fifties was the Academy Award-winning producer of "Born Free," continues to scrimmage in the notoriously competitive subculture of Hollywood. He gives me hope.

I find that I have acquired a new set of priorities. Some of the old agonies have simply disappeared. I have no doubt that my three children are more important than anything else in my life. Having achieved a certain level of worldly success, I need hardly think about it anymore. Gentler virtues seem terribly important now. I strive to be generous and productive. I would hope to be thought of as a decent and creative man.

I think Miss Shirer would be proud.

# SECTION ONE

# THE LEADERSHIP CRISIS

More than anything, the difference between a leader and a manager rests on the status quo: Managers are willing to live with it, and leaders are not.

Leaders are the ones with vision, who inspire others and cause them to galvanize their efforts and achieve change. Managers, on the other hand, will follow standard operating procedure to their graves, if necessary, because they don't possess the ability to change course.

Which do you suppose is the more important attribute to possess as we move into the next century?

The fact is, America and its business community have been managed to the edge of ruin, and now we're in desperate need of leaders. Unfortunately, it is increasingly difficult to find men and women of vision who are willing to stand on principle and make their voices heard. One has to wonder, where have all the leaders gone?

# 1

# THE LEADERSHIP CRISIS

*The colossal income gap, corporate restructuring, and
demoralized employees all spell trouble for organizations.*

In the next decade, the United States will likely experience
a period of social unrest unequaled in this century. It will
dwarf the protests of the late 1960s and early 1970s. The
recent strikes and other demonstrations in France are a por-
tent of what is to come for us.

Several things lead me to this dreary prediction:

• **The growing disparity between the rich and poor.** In
the mid '70s, the income gap between the very rich and very
poor in the U.S. was at its narrowest: One percent of the population controlled 18 percent of private wealth; now, one percent of the population controls 40 percent of the wealth.

Corporations reflect the same widening gap between the
haves and have-nots. There is a colossal disparity between the
average pay of CEOs and the pay of the average worker; estimates of the ratio range up to 140 to 1. This disparity persists
even in adverse times. While CEOs walk away from mergers
and other corporate upheavals with multimillion-dollar gold-
en parachutes, the downsized thousands get a few months'
severance pay and lose sleep over their health-care coverage.

• **The inverted trust factor.** In the mid '50s, about 70 percent of Americans believed our government was genuinely
concerned with the common good. The trust in government
eroded noisily in the mid '60s and continues to decline at an

accelerating rate. Recent studies indicate that only 25 percent of Americans now trust their government. Vice President Al Gore tells the apocryphal story of a government pollster who asked: "Do you trust the government more or less than you did five years ago?" Ten percent of those surveyed said they trusted the government more; 15 percent said they trusted it less; the remaining 75 percent refused to answer: They thought the survey was some sort of government plot.

• **The abandoned "other half."** British management philosopher Charles Handy wrote about a CEO who boasted that his equation for success was "half times two times three equals success." The CEO explained that with half the workforce he could produce twice as many goods with three times the revenues. Not bad. But, Handy asks, "What about the other half?" Most of us try to duck the question or finesse it. Some business leaders respond by talking about "employability." They say that while they can't guarantee job security, they can provide knowledge and tools for their laid-off workers to find employment elsewhere. But where is "elsewhere" these days? And who knows just what "knowledge and tools" are going to work the necessary magic in this shrinking job market?

• **Lack of empowerment.** Even the still-employed are in a chronic state of anxiety. For them, empowerment is an increasingly Orwellian term, not simply a lie, but an infuriating inversion of the truth. A demoralizing sense of powerlessness is what many jobholders are feeling. Nearly everyone worries about getting a pink slip.

How can you have empowerment in the absence of trust? The kind of trust necessary for truly creative work has become just a nostalgic memory. Empowerment and restructuring are on a collision course. It's impossible for a company to reengineer and empower at the same time, even though many firms are attempting it.

Unless the private sector finds a way both to make money and reestablish a sense of trust, we'll continue to be in trouble. Worried workers do not engage in the kind of creative problem-solving that contemporary business requires. And unless some solution is found to the dilemma facing those losing their jobs— a population segment that now includes the middle class as well as the poor—we will see public expressions of rage and fear that make the recent strikes in France look like a stroll in the park.

### The Impending Crisis

Around the globe, we currently face three extraordinary threats: the threat of annihilation as a result of nuclear accident or war, the threat of a worldwide plague or ecological catastrophe, and a deepening leadership crisis in organizations. Unlike the possibility of plague or nuclear holocaust, the leadership crisis will probably not become the basis for a best-seller or a blockbuster movie, but in many ways it is the most urgent and dangerous of the threats we face today, if only because it is insufficiently recognized and little understood.

The signs of a leadership crisis are alarming and pervasive. Witness the change in leadership at some of our most respected corporations—General Motors, IBM, and American Express. John Gardner, former Secretary of Health, Education and Welfare, acknowledges the deterioration of leadership capabilities of two of GM's former leaders, Alfred P. Sloan, Jr., and Roger Smith.

In politics, it is the same. No head of a developed, democratic nation has more than a tentative hold on his or her constituency. President Bill Clinton has an approval rating that threatens to dip below 40 percent and faces opposition from Congress unmatched in recent history. In Great Britain, John Major's Conservative government teeters. Italy and Japan must manage with interregnum governments. A recent survey taken in Canada shows that its Progressive Conservative Party, in office for a decade, has the support of only 3 percent of the population. The same poll indicates that twice as many respondents—6 percent—believe Elvis is still alive.

The leadership crisis appears to be spreading. In the United States, senators are resigning, some without encouragement of scandal. The mood of the populace is unsettled, angry, sometimes foul, and, in a few horrifying cases recently, even murderous. And those who ostensibly lead agree only that things are terrible and getting worse. Among the general population, cynicism is rampant. I don't recall such a widespread loss of faith in our major institutions even during the tumultuous 1960s. Indeed, I can't remember a time when so many of our leaders themselves were so vocally disenchanted with government, including their own political parties, as they are today.

## Three False Dichotomies

The false dichotomies mar so much of the contemporary literature about leadership. However well-intentioned, those who write about leadership have tended to become embroiled in one or more of the now familiar controversies on the subject.

Three debates, in particular, have preoccupied those concerned with leaders and leadership.

1. The first of these debates is whether leaders are larger-than-life figures—heroes who can change the weather, as Winston Churchill said his ancestor John Churchill could—or whether they are simply vivid embodiments of forces greater than themselves.

I think of this as a debate between Tolstoy and Carlyle. In Tolstoy's *War and Peace*, Napoleon and his Russian counterparts have very little to do with the ultimate outcome of the great battles with which they are identified. To use a metaphor that might have left Tolstoy tugging his beard in confusion, the leader in Tolstoy's view is just another surfer riding the waves of the zeitgeist, albeit the surfer with the biggest board.

Carlyle, on the other hand, argues that every institution is the lengthened shadow of a great man. Had he been a Southern Californian, he might have written that great leaders don't just ride waves, they make them.

2. A second false dichotomy is whether leaders are born or made. This debate is sufficiently widespread to have inspired a cartoon in which a nervous teenager presents a report card blackened with Fs to his CEO father and asks, "What do you think, Pop, genes or the environment?" To argue over nature versus nurture is an indulgent diversion from the urgent matter of how best to develop the leadership ability that so many people have and that we so desperately need. A Nobel Prize awaits the person who resolves the question of whether leaders are born or made. But for now the argument leads nowhere. The need for leadership in every arena of life has become so acute that we don't have the luxury of dwelling on the unresolvable.

3. The third of the false dichotomies is the perceived conflict between expedient and idealistic leadership. The literature on leadership uses several different terms to describe those leaders who seize the moment without regard for the impact of their actions on the quality of other people's lives. "Machiavellian" is

the harshest of these terms. The gentler ones typically crop up in discussions of contingency theory and "situationalism."

In four decades of studying leaders, I have repeatedly found them to be what I call pragmatic dreamers—men and women whose ability to get things done is often grounded in a vision that includes altruism. Thus, when Steve Jobs was recruiting John Sculley, then head of PepsiCo, for Apple Computer, Jobs knew to appeal not just to Sculley's ambition but also to his desire to leave a legacy that would go beyond boosting profit margins. Jobs is said to have asked the man who was to become Apple's next president and CEO how many more years of his life he wanted to spend making flavored water.

Scholars tackle two kinds of subjects. Some, like dry-fly fishing and the ichnography of sixteenth-century French poetry, can be plumbed to their depths. Others, like leadership, are so vast and complex that they can only be explored. The latter subjects are inevitably the more important ones.

Leadership is never exerted in a vacuum. It is always a transaction between the leader, his or her followers, and the goal or dream. A resonance exists between leaders and followers that makes them allies in support of a common cause. The leader's role in this process has been much analyzed.

My studies show, for instance, that leaders are highly focused, that they are able to inspire trust, and that they are purveyors of hope. But followers are more essential to leadership than any of those individual attributes. As Gary Wills writes in *Certain Trumpets: The Call of Leaders,* "The leader most needs followers. When those are lacking, the best ideas, the strongest will, the most wonderful smile have no effect."

Leaders are capable of deep listening: Gandhi demonstrated that when he traveled throughout India learning the heart of his people. But what distinguishes leaders from, say, psychotherapists or counselors is that they find a voice that allows them to articulate the common dream. Uncommon eloquence marks virtually every one of Gardner's leaders, but I have yet to see public speaking listed on a resume. We seem to regard the ability to galvanize an audience as something almost tawdry, even dangerous. Yet it was the eloquence of Martin Luther King, Jr., grounded in the cadences of thousands of his father's sermons, that gave him the voice of a national, even international, leader.

That fact should be kept in mind by anyone trying to draw up a curriculum for future leaders.

Effective leaders put words to the formless longings and deeply felt needs of others. They create communities out of words.

# 2

# WHERE HAVE ALL THE LEADERS GONE?

*We need some fresh faces and voices to renew organizations
and regain advantage, but we can't seem to find any.*


Franklin Roosevelt, who challenged a nation to overcome
its fears; Winston Churchill, who demanded and got blood,
sweat, and tears from his people; Albert Schweitzer, who
inspired a reverence for life; Albert Einstein, who gave us a
sense of unity in infinity; Mahatma Gandhi, David Ben-
Gurion, Golda Meir, and Anwar Sadat, who rallied their people
to great and humane causes; Jack and Bobby Kennedy and
Martin Luther King, Jr., who said we could do better—all are
gone now.

Where are their successors? Why have we not had any true
leaders in the White House in a generation? Why are there no
potential presidents who inspire or even excite us? Where, for
God's sake, have all the leaders gone?

### Short Shelf Life

In the last two decades, there has been a high turnover, an
appalling mortality—both occupational and actuarial—among
leaders. The shelf life of college presidents and CEOs has been
markedly reduced. Corporate chieftains' days at the top seem
to be numbered from the moment they take office.

In previous generations, at any given moment, there were a
half dozen university heads who were known and respected

throughout the world. James Conant, Robert Hutchins, Clark Kerr, and their like did not merely run their universities but led a kind of constant national colloquy on the state of education in America. Their turf was not simply their university but all of education, and so when they saw flaws in secondary schools, they not only pointed them out but offered solutions. I cannot remember the last time any university president addressed any problems beyond his or her own campus. Universities have changed, and so have university presidents.

In business, the landscape is equally flat. The great leaders who come to mind—Ford, Edison, Rockefeller, Morgan, Schwab, Sloan, Kettering—are long gone. Reagan's business chums are entrepreneurs outside the business establishment, such as Justin Dart, the drugstore cowboy. Other corporate heads are either organization men who have risen to the level of their incompetence, such as GM's Roger Smith; celebrities, such as Lee Iacocca; or one-man bands, such as Ted Turner, T. Boone Pickens, and Donald Trump, who devote at least as much time and energy to blowing their own horns as to business. It is no accident that the most celebrated people in business now are those who spend their days demolishing rather than creating companies.

Things are no different in politics or public service. More distinguished people announce that they will not seek the presidency than announce that they will. The problem isn't just ours. It's worldwide. No country—from here to Great Britain to Germany to Israel and Egypt—has the kind of leadership it once had and now needs more urgently than ever.

### Power and Autonomy
Never before have individuals wanted and been able to seize so much power unto themselves, and never before have they had so many tools to ensure their autonomy. The automobile, the TV, the VCR, the microwave oven, the computer all serve not only to separate us from our fellow humans but to render us independent of them. But it is the anarchic instinct that has blossomed in so many of us, not the tools, that is at the heart of the problem.

The notion of the public good, the common accord, has always been at odds with traditional American individualism, but it blew apart in the explosive 1960s, when virtually every institution came under fire. We lost our leaders, found no one to replace them, and decided to do it ourselves. We questioned everyone in authority and every institution. We formed blocks of like-minded people to agitate for what we wanted and oppose what we didn't want.

Bereft of leaders and bereaved, we turned on the managers and bureaucrats, the organization men who had reduced great private corporations to money mills and great public institutions to red tape. They had not made life easy for us, and now we were going to make life difficult for them.

As individual autonomy waxed, institutional autonomy waned. External forces impinged and imposed more and more on the perimeter of our institutions; the incessant concatenation of often contrary demands grew. The government had for decades assumed more and more power over corporations and institutions. Now the people were challenging not only the government but the corporations and institutions, too. An incessant, dissonant clamor grew.

This fragmentation, which existed in virtually every organization, marked the end not only of community, a sense of shared values and symbols, but of consensus. There was Lyndon Johnson pleading, "Come, let us reason together," at a time when all these factions scarcely wanted to be together. As Abbie Hoffman said when accused of conspiracy, "Are you kidding? We couldn't agree on lunch."

Everyone went his or her own way. No one wanted to be part of mainstream America; everyone wanted instead to be black or Chicano or a woman or a gay or a Native American. The very idea of the much-heralded "melting pot" or even a milder assimilation was suspect.

### New Alliances

A new form of politics was invented—King Caucus, who has more heads than Cerberus, and contending queens who cry "Off with their heads" as they play croquet with flamingos. It was the politics of multiple advocacies—vocal, demanding, deliberately out of sync, made up of people who were fed up with being ignored, neglected, excluded, denied, subordinated. In the 1960s, they marched. In the 1970s, they sued. The law had suddenly become the court of first resort.

Our new reliance on the courts has not only diminished the autonomy of institutions, it has threatened the autonomy of the individual. We use the law now as a weapon rather than a tool. It is less and less the basis for our common accord and more and more a primary source of our continuing discord. The confusion, ambiguity, and complexity of the law—augmented by conflicting judicial interpretations—tend toward paralysis. Worse, court judgments have begun to replace expertise as the ultimate measure.

In this new anarchic state, Americans see the law less as an instrument of protection than as an instrument of assault. We are less interested in preserving our common rights than in exercising our individual rights, and versus is now the preposition of choice. I versus you. Me versus them. We see life in an adversarial light now, and the leader as the leading adversary. We haven't just lost consensus, we've deliberately polarized ourselves. Each of us is a majority of one. I and me against the world.

Decades of organization men have spawned, perhaps inevitably, antiorganization men. Junior executives rank their fealty to their own ambitions above any loyalty to the company. And why not? Traditionally, American corporations have seen their employees as adversaries, not allies. Business with a large B is the concentrated epitome of our culture, and is inseparable from it. Environmental encroachments and turbulence, the steady beat of litigation, the fragmentation of constituencies, along with their newfound eloquence and power, multiple advocacy, conflicts between internal and external forces, and an "every man for himself" climate in the executive suites, have turned corporate chiefs into broken field runners—dodging, ducking, moving fast, and demanding "golden parachutes" to soften the inevitable fall.

More and more chiefs, aware of the rancorous mood of the Indians, play it safe and, living up to the inverted proverb, don't just do something but simply sit there. Such people avoid trouble, but they also diminish the possibility of progress. The sense of individual responsibility that animated the Constitution has vanished, as both chiefs and Indians now trumpet the new credos: It's not my job, and it's not my fault.

Newborn babies are dressed in designer diapers. Little children are pushed into boutique nursery schools, where excellence is measured by the cut of one's polo shirts. Teenagers drive VW Cabriolets and are driven to score stupendously on their SATs, so they can go to Brown and graduate to Wall Street, where the players use real money, and jail's the only limit.

Young people no longer dream of going to the moon, or even making a better mousetrap. They dream of money, and know that the best things in life—VCRs, cellular phones, Beemers, dinners at the Quilted Giraffe or Rebecca's—aren't free. They don't vote, of course, believing that politics are obsolete, along with politicians.

These days, each of us is part talent, part ambition, and part conscience. Ambition accelerates talent, while conscience controls drive and guides talent. Talent and ambition are born and bred in us and are as profoundly personal and distinctive as fingerprints. Conscience is as communal as it is personal, combining our own sense of right and wrong with the prevailing ethic. Instead of opposing this anarchic turn, far too many public- and private-sector chieftains have opted for a kind of anarchy themselves. The new corporate order disavows fidelity to employees, businesses, factories, communities, the nation, and products. The only things that count to many CEOs are market dominance, profits, and healthy stock prices, according to Steven Prokesch of the *New York Times*. Prokesch writes:

> *With this mind set, chief executives are losing interest in maintaining a favorable American trade balance, or even manufacturing in America. And they are quick to try out new operating procedures if they seem likely to be profitable. . . . The new corporate thinking casts CEOs as global warriors rather than national ones.*

In other words, nothing counts except profits, and profits count because they are the sole measure of the CEO. Conscience and competence take a backseat to ambition, as the wheel that turns the fastest gets the bonus.

### There Was a Time

There was a time when CEOs were civic leaders and corporate statesmen. Today, they have no interest in anything but their own bottom lines. The visionaries, too, are gone. Only surefire products and systems win the attention of the CEO, who has neither the time nor the inclination to commit his or her company to a potentially innovative or even useful product. If it isn't likely to be an instant best-seller, it isn't likely to get an okay. American businessmen or businesswoman never had many moral imperatives, but they did feel some obligation to their employees, the towns they operated in, and the national economy. That's no longer true. In the same way, as Prokesch says:

> *Many chief executives preach the virtues of employee involvement, teamwork and participative management, but for a calculated reason. Personnel cutbacks have taken a heavy toll on employee loyalty, which, in turn, threatens to take a toll on company efforts to bolster productivity and product quality. As a consequence, executives face the difficult paradox of having to convince employees that they really care about them— until the axe falls in the next wave of cutbacks.*

As corporate employers increasingly require their employees to sign "fire at will" clauses—statements that the employees recognize the right of the corporation to fire them "at will," for no fault of their own, for no reason but whim—the last ray of the covenant is dissolving.

Where have all the leaders gone? They're out there pleading, trotting, temporizing, putting out fires, trying to avoid too much heat. They're peering at a landscape of bottom lines. They're money changers lost in a narrow orbit. They resign. They burn out. They decide not to run or serve. They're organizational Houdinis, surrounded by sharks or shackled in a cage, always managing to escape, miraculously, to make more money via their escape clauses than they made in several years of work. They motivate people through fear, by following trends or by posing as advocates of "reality," which they cynically make up as they go along. They are leading characters in the dreamless society, given now almost exclusively to solo turns.

Thus, precisely at the time when the trust and credibility of our alleged leaders are at an all-time low and when potential leaders feel most inhibited in exercising their gifts, America most needs leaders—because, of course, as the quality of leaders declines, the quantity of problems escalates.

As a person cannot function without a brain, a society cannot function without leaders. And so the decline goes on.

# 3

## LONG SLIDE FROM
## TRUE LEADERSHIP

*We don't seem to want leaders anymore because we have
become safe and secure in our cocoons of self-interest.*

Two hundred years ago, when the nation's founders gathered in Philadelphia to write the Constitution, the United States had a population of only 3 million people, yet six world-class leaders contributed to the making of that extraordinary document. Today, there are more than 240 million of us, and we have Ollie North, the thinking man's Rambo. What happened?

As 18th century America was notable for its free-wheeling adventurers and entrepreneurs, and early 20th century America for its scientists and inventors, late 20th century America has been notable for its bureaucrats and managers.

What those Philadelphia geniuses created, and their rowdy successors built, the organization men—in both government and business—have remade, or unmade. Unlike either our nation's founders or industrial titans, the managers of America's giant corporations and the bureaucrats, elected and appointed, have no gut stake in the enterprise and no vision. More often than not, they're just hired guns, following the money.

This new breed are as cool as their predecessors were hot, analytical rather than intuitive, and careful rather than careless. More often than not, these hired guns have no vision beyond the quarterly report.

The managers agree with Calvin Coolidge, who said, "The business of America is business." Their government counterparts, the bureaucrats, see it differently. They set out to tame the big corporation in the same way that the corporations' founders had tamed the continent itself. The managers parry with lobbyists to tame Congress, and so America continues to bypass democracy in favor of government of, by, and for special interests—that is, capitalism.

As bureaucrats and managers trade favors, a stalemate develops. Nothing much grows in a stalemate, of course, but managers and bureaucrats are less gardeners than mechanics, fonder of tinkering with machinery than making things grow.

Meanwhile, the United States has lost its edge. The much-bruited American century was suddenly the Japanese century—in business, anyway. It's anyone's guess whose century it has become politically.

Things do not happen without reasons. We lost the edge because, however skillful managers and bureaucrats are at holding actions, they have no talent at all for advancing. Thus, today, America no longer leads the world, and is itself leaderless.

The national rebellion of the 1960s, the "Me Decade" that followed, yesterday's yuppies, and today's Generation X are all consequences of the mistakes and crudities of the organization men. Many of our citizens have come to see the United States as the biggest, most mindless, and clumsiest corporation of all. They can't find either its head or its heart. But, ignoring all the signals, along with their responsibilities, the managers and bureaucrats continue to flex their considerable muscle. White House underlings run covert actions in violation of the law, while corporate honchos gather their wagons in a circle in paranoid preparation for the ultimate shootout.

For all their brass, these new business kingpins are not leaders but merely bosses. Like the dinosaurs, though they may tower over their surroundings, they are not necessarily equipped for survival. These bosses confuse quantity with quality and substitute ambition for imagination. Much like Washington's tin soldiers and sunshine patriots, they do not understand the world as it is.

### Self-Interest Leadership Illusion

America has been dragged, feet first, into the late 20th century. The former Soviet Union dictates what passes for our foreign policy, along with our ruinous defense budget. The Japanese and Germans have taken over our primary totems— the automobile and the TV set. Tiny bands of terrorists regularly mug us. Unfriendly dictatorships blackmail us. And we have become the world's leading debtor nation.

Like the big old American car, America seems too big and too awkward to work very well, much less respond quickly and wisely to events. Like its big corporations, the nation seems devoted to outmoded methods and ideas that were not very good to start with and seems unwilling or unable to change direction, or even to recognize that its foreign and domestic policies are not only outdated but dangerously insufficient.

Our fundamental confusion was perfectly expressed in the presidential election of 1980 when the offspring of the once-radical movements of the 1960s found themselves in step with Ronald Reagan, the man old enough to be their grandfather, the longtime hero of and spokesperson for the far right. With him, they believed that the individual was all, and greed was everything. Self-interest was not only a virtue, it was patriotic.

Once upon a time, we all wanted to be Lindbergh or DiMaggio or Astaire, because they were the best at what they did; now we want to be Pickens, Trump, or Iacocca, because they're rich. Far too often now, our idols are all smoke and mirrors, sound and fury, signifying nothing. But they do not rise unassisted: Our need, as much as their greed, catapults them into the spotlight's golden glare.

### CorpKings and McHeroes

Our need for true leaders goes unspoken, but it manifests itself in pathetic ways—as in our idolatry of show business stars, our admiration for corporate kings, and our instant elevation of McHeroes such as Ollie North. We didn't much like what he did, but we loved the way that he did it.

The recent popularity of instant leadership courses is another symptom of this fundamental need. The courses themselves demonstrate our confusion about what constitutes leadership. Some claim it derives automatically from power. Others say it's mere mechanics—a thorough comprehension of the nature of organizations. Some say that leaders are born, while others argue that they can be made, and according to the microwave theory, made instantly. Pop in Mr. or Ms. Average, and out pops another McLeader in sixty seconds.

Billions of dollars are spent annually by and on would-be leaders, yet we have no leaders, and though many corporations now offer leadership courses to their more promising employees, corporate America has lost its lead in the world market. In fact, to this point more leaders have been made by accident, circumstances, and sheer will than have been made by all the leadership courses.

Today, we do not dream but merely fantasize about money and things. As a dreamless sleep is death, a dreamless society is meaningless. As individuals, we need dreams in the way we need air, and as a society, we need true leaders—uncommon men and women who, having invented themselves, can reinvent America and restore the collective dream by expressing for and to us that irreverent, insouciant, peculiarly American spirit.

Right now, there are probably thousands of potential leaders in America—young men and women full of passion for the promises of life with no outlets for that passion, because we scorn passion even as we reward ambition. If history is to be trusted, they are more likely than not the loners, the kids who seem always to be a little at odds with their peers, off there, looking at life from a different angle—originals, not copies.

Leaders, like anyone else, are the sum of all their experiences, but, unlike others, they amount to more than the sum, because they make more of their experiences. This is the best and worst of all possible worlds for bright, young, would-be leaders; best because their opportunities for personal achievement are unlimited, worst because America has never been less interested in achievement or more interested in success. Everyone insists on having his or her own way now.

The conflicts between individual rights and the common good are far older than the nation, but they have never been as sharp or as mean as they are today. In fact, as the "upwardly mobile" person has replaced the citizen, we have less and less in common and less and less that is good.

The founding fathers based the Constitution on the assumption that there was such a thing as public virtue. James Madison wrote, "The public good...the real welfare of the great body of people...is the supreme object to be pursued." At the moment, we not only cannot agree on what the public good is, we show no inclination to pursue it.

The notion of public virtue was replaced early on by special interests that were succeeded, in the 1960s, by what we call, vaguely, "values." Robert N. Bellah and his coauthors define values in *Habits of the Heart* as "the incomprehensible, indefensible thing that the individual chooses when he or she has thrown off the last vestige of external influence and reached pure contentless freedom." The promised Great Society of the 1960s has evolved into what Bellah and his coauthors (1985) call "a permissive therapeutic culture . . . which urges a strenuous effort to make our particular segment of life a small world of its own."

People are literally retreating into their electronic castles, working at home and communicating with the world via computers; screening their calls on answering machines; ordering in movies for their VCRs, food for their microwave ovens, and trainers for their bodies; and keeping the world at bay with advanced security systems. Trend spotters call this phenomenon "cocooning," but it might more accurately be described as terminal egocentricity.

As a nation cannot survive without virtue, it cannot progress without some common vision—and we haven't had a real sense of purpose, as a people, since the 1960s.

### Metamorphosis for Flight

A healthy, productive society is based on high expectations. The individual expects society to be virtuous, just, and productive. As the individual must continually challenge society to live up to its promises, society, at the same time, must continually encourage the individual to fulfill his or her promise. At the moment, neither the individual nor society seems interested in doing better—except on the most atavistic level. It abuses us, and we use it.

But since we are the society, we can't expect it to do better until we do better. And we will not do better until we emerge from our cocoons. We show no inclination to do that, and there is on the horizon no leader who seems capable of inspiring or moving us in a more positive direction. For those who would argue that there is Jesse Jackson, who can certainly rouse people with his vision of things as they could and should be, I must respond that he is, like Ronald Reagan, a creation of our times, one who has shown consummate understanding of both media and public. But Jackson has shown little or no steadiness, so that both his judgment and his character are called into question. Jackson preaches a better game than he practices.

No, for the moment, anyway, we don't seem to want leaders. In these mean, greedy times, we seem to prefer co-conspirators, and that is exactly what we have—in the White House, the boardrooms, even the classrooms. There is, then, no doubt that we could do better but considerable doubt as to whether we want to, and so we are destined to drift on dreamlessly, secure in our cocoons of self-interest.

# 4

## THE LEADER AS HERO

*While some people may argue that making heroes of corporate leaders is an innocent activity, I say it leads to some unhealthy idolatry.*

The captains of industry are back. It's almost impossible to pick up a book, watch television news (or "Miami Vice," for that matter, which once featured Lee Iacocca in a cameo role), or leaf through *People* magazine without getting one more report on America's celebrity executives, or the corporate chieftain as hero.

In the early 1970s, I lamented the passing of the executive superstars, but obviously reports of their demise were greatly exaggerated. And while I admit to being one of the first to shout hosanna at their reappearance, I must confess that my initial enthusiasm is now on the wane. Part of the problem is the sheer volume of uncritical adulation.

Magazines, audio and video cassettes, brochures and books extolling the virtues of corporate leadership crowd my desk. A recent issue of *Psychology Today*, for instance, reviews five books and notes they "all portray the corporate leader as teacher, mentor, exemplar and forger of values and meaning."

The books on my desk include *The Great Getty, Geneen,* Tom Peters' latest offering, subtitled *The Leadership Difference, Making It Happen* (about 1984 Summer Olympics CEO Peter Ueberroth), *CEO: Corporate Leadership in Action, The Power to Lead,* and *The Big Time* (about the extraordinarily successful Harvard Business School class of 1949).

Clearly, high-level executives are getting the full celebrity

37

treatment. In fact, my two teen-age sons, neither of whom is a business major, recognize the names of Lee Iacocca, T. Boone Pickens, Ted Turner, Armand Hammer, Steve Jobs, Harold Geneen, Victor Kiam, Frank Borman and Sandy Sigoloff—even if they couldn't name the CEO of Sears. Some of these men have become role models, ranking right up there with "The Boss," Bruce Springsteen.

What a contrast between this outpouring of adulation for our captains of industry and the universal hatred for their 19th century counterparts, the so-called robber barons. Jay Gould was known as "one of the worst stinkers in American business," and many other corporate leaders of that time suffered similar opprobrium.

### Why the Switch?

Why has the contemporary corporate leader re-emerged as an authentic American hero? There are some timely explanations.

A case can be made, for example, that galloping technology, widespread deregulation, financial and economic upheaval and social change have vastly complicated the CEO's role, while simultaneously raising the stakes and heightening his visibility.

Another, contradictory, explanation is that the present business climate is the most favorable in decades—if only because it is the most exhilarating.

A third, discouraging explanation is that, to paraphrase a popular song, we are a material people. Selfishness is suddenly respectable, and, in a nation full of people bent on acquiring status symbols, there is no higher status or more admirable symbol than the topmost rung on the corporate ladder.

A fourth, quite human, explanation is that in this volatile world, a strong, certain CEO is a far more reliable hero than, say, a rock star.

There is also a historical explanation. American cultural traditions define personality, achievement, and the purpose of human life in ways that suspend the individual in glory. The chief exponent of this tradition was Ralph Waldo Emerson, whose famous Phi Beta Kappa lecture at Harvard, "On Self-Reliance," was described by Oliver Wendell Holmes as "our intellectual Declaration of Independence."

As the major spokesman for American Transcendentalism, Emerson guided a movement that emphasized humanism and the spiritual self. Upon leaving the Unitarian church, in which he was an ordained minister, he made individualism his religion, ignoring the obvious dangers. Emerson meant to give people courage to be, to follow their own instincts, but his notion became the platform for American enterprise and a philosophical license for corporate tycoons. To this day, and especially today, we're drawn to powerful individuals, and there are no more powerful individuals among us than the captains of industry.

### What's So Bad?

What's so bad about feeling good about these corporate superstars? Plenty. Inarguably, cults develop around such leaders, which is an unhealthy situation for both the leader and his or her followers. The leader begins to believe in his or her own infallibility, and people who believe they can do no wrong are a menace to themselves as well as to the rest of us. Idolatry turns people into lackeys, who are so mesmerized by their idol's talents that they neglect their own. Then, too, they are so eager to do their leader's bidding that they don't bother to measure whether what they are doing is right or wrong.

The bureaucratization of imagination is inevitable. In a way, everyone puts his or her own mind on hold, and accepts the dicta of the leader as absolute. The only worthy ideas are the ideas of the leader, or mirror images of his or her ideas. Sooner or later, the company finds itself trying to run on empty.

No matter how wise, shrewd or visionary a leader is, a corporation is a collective endeavor, and it needs the collective wisdom, canniness, and vision of all of its employees to function at the optimum level.

These corporate stars eclipse not only their subordinates, but the competition. When they move on, or retire, their companies suffer months, even years, of instability, while they search for someone who can truly fill their leader's outsized shoes. Furthermore, these corporate stars, like their show business counterparts, are inclined toward star turns, including the false retirement and inevitable comeback. CBS's William Paley has retired several times, and yet returned to the helm of the network, to the eternal dismay of several "successors."

But even when the star does not rise again and again, like some eternal phoenix, the company is in for some turbulence, as it strains to turn what was a one-man show into a fully functional organization. A monarchy differs from a republic in fundamental ways, and the departed ruler's minions are left with the complex task of picking up the pieces and re-assembling them along less autocratic lines.

Whoever succeeds the star faces a herculean task. If he has inclinations toward stardom himself, he has to erase even the memory of his predecessor overnight, as, in this instance, he who hesitates for even a moment is bound to lose face. If, on the other hand, he chooses the path of effective leadership, he will find the path strewn with hazards, such as executives who have forgotten how to make decisions on their own, a rusted chain of command, and plenty of unfinished business.

In such cases, the mortality rate of successors is very high. An organization may go through several new CEOs before it finds one who can restore its stability and get it back on course.

All the idolatry tends, too, to go to the corporate star's head, and he or she begins to behave like a mini-emperor, inclined to get rid of anyone who dissents or has a better idea. Too, mini-emperors naturally have imperial tastes and habits, which tend to cost the company dearly. They expect perks that would dazzle a sheik, demand services that are above and beyond the call of both duty and reason, and expect mega-bonuses whether or not the company has gained or lost during his or her reign. Even after such people have left the company, the company often goes right on paying them, in the form of yearly stipends, bonuses and stock. Ironically, the less well someone's done, the more they're apt to profit, as the company is often forced to literally buy them off. Ex-American presidents' perks pale when compared to these regal settlements.

Finally, there is the Oz factor. Far too often these corporate potentates are empty suits, all sound and show signifying nothing. This particular breed of star is generally hired under the misapprehension that his name or face will bring fame, attention and adulation to the company. But it's a bad bargain, as the cost of such a show often exceeds the benefits. Such figureheads too often lack the kind of experience and knowledge that the corporation requires in its top spot, with the result that it finds itself fumbling while the whole world is watching.

High visibility has absolutely nothing to do with getting the job done. For example, the no-name executive team at Ford consistently outclasses the stars at Chrysler and General Motors.

This is not to say that celebrity and performance are mutually exclusive. As in show business, it is frequently the case that talent has little or nothing to do with the star's ascension, and that, whether talented or not, the mere presence of a star can radically alter whatever arena he or she inhabits, turning otherwise capable associates into fans and skewing everyone's priorities.

But, of course, these corporate nabobs did not rise to the heights on their own. As I said in the beginning, it was our need as much as their ambition that catapulted them into the spotlight's golden glare. In trying to restore some balance, then, we must overcome our own need for omnipotent heroes along with our heroes' appetite for adulation.

Here, time and circumstances may be on the side of reason. Currently, the burnout rate for such corporate stars is very high, so the day may not be far off when corporations stop being one-man shows and become team efforts again.

# 5

# Untapped Human Capital

*Unless leaders learn to value their people and tap the potential of their human resources, their organizations will sink.*

Louis B. Mayer, the head of MGM Studios during Hollywood's golden era, was known for his tyrannical habits, yet he made MGM into a pivotal cultural force, shaping the movies that shaped America. He knew what today's corporate titans either never know or can't accept—that the only capital that really counts is human capital.

Mayer once said, "The inventory goes home at night," conceding that without his corps of talented directors, writers, and actors, MGM would be nothing. In the same way, whatever a modern corporation markets—from cars to meals to life insurance—its primary resource is its people. This is a basic economic fact, and our refusal to accept and act on it accounts, to a large degree, for our poor performance in the international marketplace.

American business has traditionally seen its workers in an adversarial light, as mere cogs in the corporate machine: necessary, perhaps, but anonymous, replaceable, and greedy. In the first decades of the Industrial Revolution, workers were treated as indentured servants. Finally, of course, the workers rebelled, and by the middle of this century an uneasy peace was established, with unions and businesses in an approximate, though rancorous, balance. But today, there is far more rancor than balance.

Former president Ronald Reagan expressed the basic animosity that too many CEOs feel toward both unions and workers when he fired the air traffic controllers. Nobody plays a more crucial role in airline operations than air traffic controllers. Our lives are literally in their hands, but President Reagan saw them as expendable and got rid of them, because they dared to ask for salaries that were commensurate with their responsibilities.

As the president went, so went corporate America. We have entered into a period of union bashing that is unprecedented. In the 1980s, workers were not only undervalued, but scapegoats. As American business lost its comfortable edge in the international market, American executives blamed allegedly lazy and careless workers—when, in fact, the problems resided, for the most part, in the executive suites. American executives had themselves become lazy and careless.

### Bottom-Line Obsessions

American big business's obsession with the bottom line in the last decade and its continuing inability to see that its workers are its primary asset has gotten it into big trouble.

The bottom line wasn't everything, it was the only thing. Profits mattered more than products. Making money was more important than making quality goods. It wasn't until profits began to decline that American executives even noticed that something had gone awry, and then, in time-honored fashion, they began laying off workers and shutting down plants.

They had not enough vision to see that they were losing to their overseas competition because their products, not their workers, were inferior, and their products were inferior because they devoted far more energy to making short-term profits than to developing innovative, functional and useful products. Now they are nearly out of the game. America still leads in research and development, thanks to its natural store of talented, imaginative workers, but it trails in manufacturing and marketing, thanks to a lack of talent and imagination in the executive suites.

The most impressive R&D now goes on in small new companies, which have replaced the traditional adversarial posture with a freewheeling cooperative spirit. These successful new companies are run not like feudal estates, in which workers are expected to be seen and never heard, but like roundtables, in which workers not only are expected to speak up but are assured of a receptive audience. In this way, all the talents of all the workers are tapped and used to the benefit of everyone, including customers.

Moreover, these businesses are profitable and are adding workers even as Fortune 500 companies are losing money and laying off workers. Like Mayer, the heads of these young companies know that their primary resource is people. They understand that healthy, spirited people are the primary source of economic growth. Since 1928, the principal source of new or added national income has been human resources. Power and profit used to reside in property. Now they reside in people. Productivity, that key measure in both companies and nations, is attributable less to the quantity of their resources than to the quality of their people.

Everyone seems to understand this fundamental fact of business life except our business titans. In a pastoral letter entitled "Economic Justice for All," the National Conference of Catholic Bishops showed more business savvy than many CEOs. Noting that "The promise of the American dream—freedom for all persons to develop their God-given talents to the full—remains unfulfilled for millions in the United States today," and concerned about the "social fragmentation, a decline in seeing how one's work serves the whole community," the bishops called for "new forms of cooperation and partnership and participation within firms."

But, the bishops warned, "Partnerships between labor and management are possible only when both groups possess real freedom and power to influence decisions."

Such partnerships, however sensible, seem unlikely. Even in the young, successful companies, we already see signs of the traditional hierarchical habits cropping up. As these small new companies grow, they look more and more like the big old companies, and the same old schisms develop between bosses and workers. One can only conclude that the American executive is uniquely susceptible to hubris. It seems to come with the territory.

If these arrogant American chieftains do not begin to see the world as it is, do not finally acknowledge that their employees are their primary asset, not their primary liability, then all their jealously held power, prerogatives and perks will sooner or later count for nothing, because their companies will be acquired, merged, or sunk.

# 6

## QUITTING ON PRINCIPLE

*The ethical thing to do may well be to quit your job on the basis of moral principle and go out shouting.*

What do you do when the leader is wrong? Not just mistaken or slightly off base in his or her judgment, but *wrong*?

I first seriously considered the question of resignation and other expressions of dissent in spring 1970. At that time, I had just resigned as acting executive vice president of the State University of New York, Buffalo, in protest against what I considered undue use of force on the part of the acting president in dealing with a series of student strikes on campus.

My decision to resign was a turning point—the first time in many years that I was able to say, "No, I cannot allow myself to be identified with this policy," the first time I risked being an outsider rather than trying to work patiently within the system for change. My reason for resigning was an intensely personal one. I did not want to say after the police came onto the campus, "Well, I was against that move at the time."

But in my case, resigning turned out to be a remarkably ineffective form of protest for many reasons, notably my decision to retain another position while resigning the acting post. The distinction between the positions was clear only to other members of the administration, and the public interpreted my equivocal exit as a halfhearted protest.

My experience is hardly unique. Most large organizations have well-oiled mechanisms for neutralizing dissent, and employees quickly learn that bureaucracies do not tolerate dissent. These people can then capitulate. Or they can remain inside and try to win the majority over to their own position, enduring the frustration and ambiguity that go with this option. Remaining can be an excruciating experience of public loyalty and private doubt. But what of resigning? Superficially, resignation seems an easy out, but it also has its dark side. And if resignation is the choice, the problem of how to leave remains.

The garden-variety resignation is an innocuous act, no matter how righteously indignant the individual who tenders it. The act is made innocuous by a set of conventions that few resignees are able (or willing) to break. When the properly socialized dissenter resigns, he or she tiptoes out. A news release is sent to the media: "We accept with regret the resignation of . . . " it reads. The pro forma statement rings pure tin in the discerning ear, but this is the accepted ritual. One retreats under a canopy of smiles, with verbal bouquets and exchanges, however insincere, of mutual respect. The last official duty of the departing one is to keep his or her mouth shut. The rules of play require that the last word goes to those who remain inside.

The purpose served by this convention is purely institutional. Resignation is usually a sign of disharmony and possibly real trouble. But without candid follow-up, it is an empty gesture. The organization reasons, usually correctly, that the muffled troublemaker will soon be forgotten. With the irritant gone, the organization pursues its chosen course, subject only to the casual and untrained scrutiny of the general public.

Cohesiveness results from a commonly held set of values, beliefs, norms and attitudes, often summed up as culture. And those who do not share the common point of view are by definition deviant, marginal outsiders. Ironically, this pervasive emphasis on harmony does not serve organizations well. Unanimity leads rather quickly to stagnation, which, in turn, invites change by non-evolutionary means. The fact that the deviant who sees things differently may be the company's vital and only link with some new, more apt paradigm does not make the organization value that person any more. Most organizations would rather risk obsolescence than make room for non-conformists.

This is most true when the issues involved are of major importance (or when important people have taken a very strong or a personal position). When it comes to war or peace, life or death, growth or stagnation, fighting or withdrawing, reform or status quo—dissent is typically seen as fearful. Exactly at that time when it is most necessary to consider the possible consequences of a wide range of alternatives, a public show of consensus becomes an absolute value to be defended no matter what the human cost.

### Voice and Exit

Unanimity, or at least its public show, is so valued within the organizational context that it often carries more weight with an individual than his or her own conscience. The classic dilemma is when a person suddenly finds himself or herself opposed to his or her superior and colleagues in regard to some policy. If the issue at stake is important and the dissenter adamant, the gulf begins to widen.

• **Voice.** At first, the dissenter tries to exert all possible influence over the others, tries to bring others around. In his classic book, *Exit, Voice and Loyalty*, Albert O. Hirschman calls this the option of voice. Short of calling a press conference, this option can be exercised in several ways, from simply grumbling to threatening to resign. Usually the individual gives voice to his or her dissatisfaction in a series of private confrontations.

• **Exit.** When these fail, as they usually do, the dissenter must face the possibility of resigning (the option of exit). Resigning becomes a reasonable alternative as soon as voice begins to fail. The individual realizes that hours of sincere, patient argument have come to nothing, that his or her influence is waning, and so, probably, is his or her loyalty. If the individual stays on, he or she risks becoming an organizational eunuch, an individual of no influence publicly supporting a policy against his or her will, judgment, personal value system, and professional code.

As bleak as this prospect is, exit on matters of principle is still a distinctly uncommon response to institutional conflict. What accounts for our national reluctance to resign and our willingness, when forced to take the step, to settle for a "soft exit," without clamor, without a public statement of principle, and ideally without publicity?

Tremendous pressures and personal rationalizations work to dissuade the dissident from exit in favor of voice. Most of us would much rather convince the boss or top group to see "reason" than to quit. Resignation is defiant, an uncomfortable posture for most of us. Worse, it smacks of failure, the worst of social diseases among the achievement oriented. So, instead of resigning, we reason that the organization could go from bad to worse if we resigned. This may be the most seductive rationalization of all. Meanwhile, we become more deeply implicated in the policy that we silently oppose, making extrication progressively more difficult.

There are selfish reasons for resigning quietly. Most resignees would like to work again. Speaking out is not likely to enhance one's marketability. A negative aura haunts the visibly angry resignee, while the person who leaves a position ostensibly to return to business, family, teaching, or research reenters the job market without any such cloud. Many resignees prefer a low profile simply because they are aware that issues change. Why undermine one's future effectiveness by making a noisy but ineffectual stand?

However selfish the reasons, the organization reaps the major benefits when a person resigns quietly. A decorous exit conceals the underlying dissension, and the fact of resignation and the reasons behind it are subordinated to the issue of institutional face-saving. A frank resignation is regarded by the organization as an act of betrayal. Because a discreet resignation amounts to no protest at all, a soft exit lifts the opprobrium of organizational deviation from the resignee. But "hard" or "soft," exit remains the option of last resort in organizational life. Remarkably, the individual who is deeply opposed to some policy often opts for public acquiescence and private frustration.

What is it about organizations that makes it possible for people to work toward an ultimately immoral end without an immediate sense of personal responsibility or guilt? Organizations are systems of increased differentiation and specialization, and the morality of the organization is the morality of segmented acts. This environment encourages indifference and evasion of responsibility; thus, an individual can easily develop tunnel vision, concentrating on the task at hand and completing it with a sense of accomplishment, however sinister the collective result of all those jobs well done.

### Raised on Folklore

Most CEOs are raised on organizational folklore—one of the central myths being that the show of unanimity is always desirable. That this belief is false and even dangerous does not limit its currency. Yes, there are times when discretion is required. Clearly, organizations should not constantly fight in public. But what is gained by forbidding at all costs and at all times any emotional give-and-take between colleagues? Why must a person who has an honest difference of opinion with the organizational powers be silenced or domesticated or driven out so that the public can continue to believe—falsely—that organizational life is without strife? And yet organizations continue to assume the most contrived postures to maintain the illusion of harmony—postures such as lying to the public.

Our inability to transcend the dangerous notion that we don't wash our dirty linen in public verges on the schizophrenic. It implies not only that dissent is bad but that our organizations are made up not of human beings but of saints who never engage in such vulgar and offensive activities.

In fact, organizations are vulgar, sweaty, plebeian; if they are to be viable, they must create an institutional environment where a fool can be called a fool and all actions and motivations are duly and closely scrutinized for the inevitable human flaws and failures. In a democracy, meanness, dullness, and corruption are always amply represented. They are not entitled to protection from the same rude challenges that such qualities must face in the "real" world. When banal politeness is assigned a higher value than accountability or truthfulness, the result is an Orwellian world where the symbols of speech are manipulated to create false realities.

### Loyalty

All the pressures against registering dissent can be subsumed under the clumsy label of loyalty, often given as a reason or pretext for muffling dissent. In fact, they represent much more subtle personal and organizational factors, including deep-rooted psychological dependence, authority problems, simple ambition, co-optive mechanisms (the "devil's advocacy" technique), pressure to be a member of the club and fear of being outside looking in, adherence to the myth that gentlemen settle their differences amicably and privately, fear of disloyalty in the form of giving comfort to "the enemy," and, very often, that powerful Prospero aspiration: the conviction that one's own "reasonable" efforts will keep things from going from bad to worse.

Often, our real loyalty is to the code of the "organizational society" in which most of us live out our entire careers. More than 90 percent of the employed population of North America works in formal organizations. Status, position, a sense of competence and accomplishment are all achieved in our culture through belonging to these institutions. What you do determines, to a large extent, what you are. "My son, the doctor" is not only the punch line of a thousand Jewish jokes, it is a neat formulation of a significant fact about American culture. Identification with a profession or organization is a real-life passport to identity, to selfhood, to self-esteem. You are what you do, and work in our society is done in large, complex, bureaucratic structures. If one leaves the organization, particularly with protest, one is nowhere, like a character in a Beckett play—without role, without the props of office, without ambience or setting.

In fact, a few more resignations would be good for individual consciences and good for the country. I think it is important for everyone in a decision-making position in any organization to speak out. And if we find it impossible to continue as executives because we are at total and continuous odds with the organization, then I think we must quit and go out shouting.

# 7

# LEADERSHIP PORNOGRAPHY AND OPTIONAL ETHICS

*Too much distance makes leadership—like pornography—
just a mechanical act.*

When the *Pentagon Papers* were published over government objections in the early 1970s, what disturbed me even more than the deceits, the counter-deceits, the moral numbness and ethical short-circuiting of our leaders was the pornography of it all: the hubris of those men in the White House and the Pentagon, thousands of miles away from Vietnam, making life-and-death decisions for others, manipulating the most modern tools of technology, using game theory with models so abstract they could reproduce one another in one joyless, screaming parthenogenetic act—but not once could these men experience the epiphany of childbirth or the smell of burning flesh.

### Mechanical Acts
I thought of pornography because that also is distanced from reality, from direct experience. Actors in porn films are not real people making love but appendages of sexual organs engaged in mechanical acts. These appendages are so without personalities or identifiable social characteristics that, as one movie critic pointed out, they are more about physical engineering than love—just so many pistons and valves. Loveless

sex. Distant, remote, calculated, vicarious. The "war room" at
the Pentagon is as distant from the reality of war as downtown
Boston's "combat zone," the festooned area for porno sales, is
from the reality of sex.

In the *Pentagon Papers,* we see Secretary of Defense Robert S.
McNamara busying himself with the minutiae of war planning,
because lists of numbers and cost estimates have a distracting if
illusory moral neutrality. Toward the end of his tenure, he stops
questioning the military or political significance of sending
206,000 more troops into Indochina, into a war he now knows
cannot be won, and concentrates instead on the logistical problems of getting them there. There's administration. And his wife
reports that, as he fulfilled the requirements of efficiency and
effectiveness during his own final days, he began to grind his
teeth—every night—while tossing fitfully.

The so-called "good Nazi" (certainly an oxymoron) Albert
Speer elevated the promises of Hitler's "technocracy" to a point
where those promises quickly became shields against any inclination to think of the human and social consequences of his
actions. The challenges, the deadlines, the deadly routines of
the Third Reich—as of the Defense Department or any large
bureaucracy—become tasks to be performed, power to be exercised, problems to be solved, monuments to be designed (or
demolished).

Is it the nature of large-scale organizations that makes it possible for an ethical person such as McNamara to work toward
an ultimately immoral end without an immediate sense of personal responsibility or guilt? Bureaucracies are, by definition,
systems of increased differentiation and specialization, and
thus the ultimate morality of bureaucracy is the amorality of
segmented acts.

On the first real day of spring 1976, when I was president of
the University of Cincinnati, two beautiful trees in the infancy
of bloom were chopped down to make more room for cars to
turn down a campus driveway. Everybody was outraged.
Students packed into my office to tell me about it. A few were
hysterical and crying. I left my office and walked over to the little grass plot, where I saw a man with a small handsaw, clean-
ing and stacking up the milk-white wood into neat piles.

A crowd of some 200 students and faculty stood around,

and, as I broke through the circle to speak to the man with the saw, I heard hissing. He said, "Man, am I glad you're here. They're ready to crucify me." It turned out that he wasn't employed by the university but worked for a local contractor. I never found out who was responsible: the landscape artist who designed the new plot with poodle hedges or his boss, the landscape architect; the director of planning or his boss, the head of the physical plant; the vice president for management and finance, the university building committee or the executive vice president. When I called them all together, they numbered twenty, and they were innocents all. All of us. Bureaucracies are beautiful mechanisms for the evasion of responsibility and guilt. Too far from the classroom, from the battlefield, from the people, from love. That's pornography.

There are no easy answers—or options. The problem is immense and invades all of our lives. According to the Census Bureau, in the 1980s fewer than two percent of us were self-employed. Everyone else worked in large organizations. (Fortunately this is changing rapidly in the 1990s, as approximately fifteen percent are now self-employed.) In the 1900s, it was the opposite ratio. And it is simplistic and unrealistic to talk about "small is beautiful," as we learned in the 1970s. Smallness helps only if it prevents the episodic, disconnected experience that characterizes so many of our leaders and administrators, but it usually doesn't, because increasingly they are the products of bigness.

Nor does it solve anything when a leader pretends closeness to or a direct relationship with the people, as when Jimmy Carter wore jeans and cardigan sweaters in the White House. The "simple" life—as seen on a technetronic quadraphonic TV tube—is soft porn for the intellectual, falsely soothing and just as corrupt as the hard kind.

What's important is the capacity to see things in wide perspective, to receive impressions and gain experiences directly, not vicariously, impressions that point beyond the experiences and data themselves—continuity and purpose.

To the pornographic leader, things and events of the world appear as portable fragments. The long view is replaced by shortsightedness. There is detail but no pattern. The fresh outlook yields to a stereotyped and biased one. Experiences and impressions, what there are of them seen through the Lucite gray of a limousine window, cannot be fully valued and enjoyed because their character—their feel, their smell, their grit—is lost.

One reason why many executives *seem* so out of touch with the real world is that they *are* out of touch—insulated by position, money, and circumstance from what really goes on inside the organization. Our leaders must reacquaint themselves with the world, must explore in the presence of others, must reach out and touch the people they presume to lead, and must, occasionally at least, risk making a mistake rather than doing nothing. In the meantime, they will continue to sound as if they were talking through a plate-glass window—distant, isolated, removed from the complex lives of living people.

### Let Virtues Shine Through

Humanity has walked on the moon, has hurled a satellite 600 million miles into space to send back telephotos of Jupiter, has conquered disease and ignorance, and has raised a remarkable number of people to a standard of living that by medieval standards is truly regal. Individuals have produced brilliant works of art that inspire and instruct us. We have, it would seem, advanced to a degree that our ancestors could not even have imagined. But they probably could not have imagined our foolishness either—our profligate waste of the earth's resources, our continuing devotion to war as a means of settling disputes, our investing billions in weapons we claim we won't use, our apparent inability to educate our young people and care humanely for the poor, the sick, and the elderly, our addiction to drugs, and, perhaps most of all, our appalling ignorance of ourselves.

It is the nature of Americans to hope. André Maurois said we were, "in a word, optimists." I am, obviously, an optimist or I wouldn't have spent my life striving to find ways for us to use ourselves better and more fully. Each of us is, in a sense, a miser who has vast resources that he or she hoards rather than spends. Even a genius uses, at most, only 80 percent of his or her potential. Few of us use even 50 percent, and, in these fast, mean times, we seem unwilling to use our best qualities at all.

Our best qualities are integrity, dedication, magnanimity, humility, openness, and creativity. These, of course, are the basic ingredients of leadership, and our unwillingness to tap these qualities in ourselves explains, to a large extent, the leadership shortage.

By *integrity,* I mean standards of moral and intellectual honesty on which our conduct is based. Without integrity, we betray ourselves and others and cheapen every endeavor. It is the single quality whose absence we feel most sharply on every level of our national life. But the nation's integrity will be restored only when each of us asserts his or her own integrity. By their very existence, people of integrity lend hope to our innate conviction that we, as a people, can rise above the current moral cynicism and squalor. As Aristotle wrote in *Ethics,* "If you would understand virtue, observe the conduct of virtuous men." Integrity, like charity, begins at home. Only when each of us asserts his or her own integrity will it be restored to the nation.

By *dedication,* I mean a passionate belief in something. This sort of intense and abiding commitment is the basis for great works of art, inventions, scientific discoveries, explorations, and lives. It is what makes marriages, corporations, and governments work. Indeed, absolute fidelity to someone or something makes us more fully human.

Human beings cannot live wholly and fully without giving themselves without reservation to something beyond themselves. Dedicated citizens do not simply write letters to their representatives in Congress, they involve themselves at the grass roots level in politics and work actively for the causes they support. In the same way, they do not simply deplore the plight of the homeless, they do whatever they can to alleviate their plight. Dedicated workers—whether they sell insurance or write novels or run corporations—not only do better work, they do it joyfully.

By *magnanimity,* I mean being "noble of mind and heart; generous in forgiving; above revenge or resentment." In the midst of the Civil War, with the fate of the Union in his hands, Abraham Lincoln called at the home of General George McClellan, found him out, and waited an hour with his secretary, John Hay. When McClellan came home and was told that Lincoln was waiting, he sent word that he had retired for the evening. Lincoln left, with Hay fuming at McClellan's insolence.

Lincoln said, "I will hold McClellan's horse if he will bring us a victory." That's magnanimity. It's also akin to humility.

Magnanimous and humble people are notable for their self-possession. They know who they are, have healthy egos, and take more pride in what they do than in who they are. They take compliments with a grain of salt and take intelligent criticism without rancor. Such people learn from their mistakes and don't harp on the mistakes of others. They are gracious winners and losers. Tennis star John McEnroe is neither magnanimous nor humble. Albert Schweitzer and Albert Einstein were. Today, there are far more McEnroes than there are Schweitzers and Einsteins, and self-possession declines as self-importance rises. True leaders are, by definition, both magnanimous and humble.

By *openness,* I mean a willingness to try new things and hear new ideas, however bizarre, a tolerance for ambiguity and change, and a rejection of any and all preconceived prejudices, biases, and stereotypes. The open-minded person does not rank people according to race, color, religion, or occupation; does not measure ideas on the basis of their source; will eat or drink virtually anything once, including snake meat; will read unknown, uncelebrated writers; listen to his or her children's CDs; and watch performance artists doing eccentric things. Open-mindedness does not make such a person critical, but it does inspire him or her to be both adventurous and creative.

We seem to lose our creativity, or at least let it atrophy, as we grow up. This is too bad, as every child under ten is not only creative but original, while most adults not only are uncreative but are copies of other adults. Stand outside any urban office building in the morning and count the number of men not wearing the usual pinstripes or gray worsted suit with the mandatory power tie, which is, at the moment, yellow. These people make a lot of money and have a lot of responsibility, yet they lack either the creativity or the courage to choose suits that are different from all the other suits. Unfortunately, their minds are generally as conventional as their garb.

*Creativity* is something that we are all born with and that almost all of us manage to lose. We don't really see the world around us. We may see a flower but not the miracle of it, its intricate structure, its complete harmony, its amazing colors. To restore our creativity, we must restore our sense of wonder, break through our own preconceptions and see everything new and fresh—as we did when we were children. This means making the familiar strange and making the strange familiar.

The more our work makes us specialists, the more we must strive to remain or become generalists in other matters, to perceive the interconnections between science, esthetics, and ethics, to avoid becoming lopsided. All of humanity's pursuits are connected, after all, and we remain ignorant of those connections at our peril.

The surgeon, the CEO, the account executive, the broker all need to know as much as they can about everything if they want to understand anything. Robots and computers can do virtually everything people can do now, but they cannot be creative, which, at bottom, might be defined as thinking for yourself. Einstein once said, "The most incomprehensible thing about the universe is that it is comprehensible." Creative people strive to comprehend as much as they can of it, to truly see, hear, and understand, to connect, and to make something worthy out of all that.

Integrity, dedication, magnanimity, humility, openness, and creativity—or, more succinctly, vision and virtue—are in all of us, however rusty or dormant they may be. Anyone who intends to lead us out of the current slough will have to exercise both.

### Optional Ethics

Sometimes there seem to be no innocents left in America. Ollie North claimed to be a patriot, but his patriotism resulted in a home security system and a numbered Swiss bank account. Teenagers peddle drugs on the streets in East Los Angeles. Self-proclaimed men of God recite the Ten Commandments on Sundays and break them the other six days of the week. Spying for dollars is our latest growth industry, and Wall Street looks more and more like a branch of Sing Sing.

In the late 1960s, yippies were political activists. In the 1980s, yippies were young indicted professionals, while yuppies, our grand acquisitors, consumed by consumption, turned out to be young unindicted professionals—those who hadn't got caught yet. They didn't vote, of course, believing that politics were obsolete, along with politicians.

Gary Hart made himself obsolete by denying that he was a womanizer, then womanizing and claiming he hadn't. When faced with further evidence of his womanizing, he quit the race for the Democratic presidential nomination and suggested that he was too good for us. The American people seemed as confused as Hart himself as to what he had done wrong. Was he brought down because he allegedly committed adultery or because he allegedly lied? Or was it because he was too proud and too arrogant? Or was he simply guilty of bad judgment?

The traditionalists objected most to his alleged adultery. The more modern among us could excuse Hart's purported sin of adultery on the grounds that what a man does in the bedroom is no one's business. But we were bothered by his apparent lies.

The hippest and most contemporary citizens dismissed the charges of both adultery and lying, because after all everyone who is anyone does both, but they saw Hart's bad judgment as his fatal flaw. In other words, they weren't bothered by what he did, but that he got caught. I didn't find anyone who was disturbed by Hart's hubris. Once upon a time, pride was a sin. Now it's a virtue.

Our national confusion over Hart's alleged mistakes vividly demonstrates a startling ethical decline. It is not simply that more of us are engaging in unethical behavior, it is because more and more we are unwilling or unable to identify or define what constitutes unethical behavior.

After Wall Street trader Ivan Boesky was nailed, a TV news crew went into a Wall Street bar and interviewed some young traders. Each and every one expressed admiration for Boesky and contempt for the Securities and Exchange Commission. Earlier, when four of their own were caught playing games that were too fast and loose even for Wall Street, the disgraced young traders were more censured than pitied. Winning isn't everything, it's the only thing, and getting caught is for losers. And, as one market analyst said, it isn't a bull market or a bear market, "it's a pig market."

After another round of arrests on the Street, an investment banker told the *New York Times* that the sight of their colleagues in handcuffs "put the fear of God in everybody." Such late-inning invocations are, of course, S.O.P. for white-collar felons, as we saw in the wake of Watergate. And why not? Almost anyone would rather wear a halo than handcuffs. But, as the revelations about Jim and Tammy Bakker and their PTL (Praise the Lord) Club showed, the church was no holier than Wall Street, and was at least as profitable.

Ollie North's exercise in patriotism for profit, Wall Street's dirty dozen, Hart's fall, the Bakkers' highly secular adventures are manifestations of a social crisis of enormous proportions.

In this highly materialistic nation, the prevailing ethic is, at best, pragmatic, and, at worst, downright dishonest. It's every man for himself, and never mind God, country, or anything else. There seems to be no such thing as the common good or the public interest. Only self-interest. The old entrepreneurial spirit that Ronald Reagan admired so ardently is running amuck, and the country is coming unstuck.

Ted Turner buys MGM and guts it. GE gobbles up RCA while the airlines feed on each other. TV evangelists squeeze big bucks out of believers, and Wall Street traders and Washington patriots peddle their services to the highest bidders. The rich get richer, and the poor get poorer. And the federal deficit gets bigger. As the poet William Butler Yeats said in another time and place, "the center is not holding."

It is time, then, to face this ethical deficit or America will end in shambles. Ethics and conscience aren't optional. They are the glue that binds society together—the quality in us that separates us from cannibals. Without conscience and ethics, talent and power amount to nothing.

# SECTION TWO

# WHAT MAKES A LEADER?

To survive in the 21st century, we're going to need a new generation of leaders—*leaders*, not managers.

The distinction is an important one. Leaders conquer the context—the volatile, turbulent, ambiguous surroundings that sometimes seem to conspire against us and will surely suffocate us if we let them—while managers surrender to it. There are other differences, as well, and they are crucial:

- The manager administers; the leader innovates.
- The manager is a copy; the leader is an original.
- The manager maintains; the leader develops.
- The manager relies on control; the leader inspires trust.
- The manager has a short-range view; the leader has a long-range perspective.
- The manager asks how and when; the leader asks what and why.
- The manager has his or her eye on the bottom line; the leader has his or her eye on the horizon.
- The manager accepts the status quo; the leader challenges it.
- The manager is the classic good soldier; the leader is his or her own person.
- The manager does things right; the leader does the right thing.

Field Marshal Sir William Slim led the 14th British Army from 1943 to 1945 in the reconquest of Burma from the Japanese—one of the epic campaigns of World War II. He recognized the distinction between leaders and managers when he said:

*Managers are necessary; leaders are essential. Leadership is of the spirit, compounded of personality and vision. Management is of the mind, more a matter of accurate calculation, statistics, methods, timetables, and routine.*

I spent ten years talking with leaders, including Jim Burke at Johnson & Johnson, John Sculley at Apple, television producer Norman Lear, and close to 100 other men and women, some famous and some not. In the course of my research, I learned something about the current crop of leaders and something about the leadership that will be necessary to forge the future. While leaders come in every size, shape, and disposition—short, tall, neat, sloppy, young, old, male and female—every leader I talked with shared at least one characteristic: a concern with a guiding purpose, an overarching vision. They were more than goal-directed. As the late aerialist Karl Wallenda said, "Walking the tightwire is living; everything else is waiting."

Leaders have a clear idea of what they want to do—personally and professionally—and the strength to persist in the face of setbacks, even failures. They know where they are going and why.

But leaders don't just appear out of thin air. They must be developed—nurtured in such a way that they acquire the qualities of leadership.

# 8

# MR. WRIGHT IS WRONG

*The story of Mr. Tinker and Mr. Wright illustrates the difference between an entrepreneurial leader and dutiful manager.*

When General Electric took over RCA, it was comparable to a whale swallowing another whale. GE had had impressive performance over the years, but RCA had not only had an equally impressive run, it was, thanks to its highly visible subsidiary NBC, better-known and more influential than GE.

A few years prior, NBC had been a wreck of a network. But it did win the 1985–86 rating wars, easily beating ABC, along with the once-imperial CBS, and repeated its stunning performance in the 1986–87 season. It took nearly every week, leading runner-up CBS by two full rating points, which translates into approximately three million homes, and millions of dollars in advertising revenues.

To its further credit, NBC made this impressive advance not by pandering to the worst in its audience, but by challenging it with new kinds of programming, often brilliantly conceived and wrought. It managed to combine financial success with substantive product innovations and improvements.

The principal architect of NBC's amazing renaissance was Grant Tinker, who left the network shortly after GE took over. Ironically, his successor Robert Wright—a longtime GE hand—seemed determined, at the very least, to pluck the peacock. Shortly after taking over, he asked each network division to come up with a plan to reduce its budget by five percent. That's standard operating procedure for GE, whose CEO, Jack Welch, is called Neutron Jack, because when he finishes "streamlining" a company, the buildings remain, but the people are gone.

Unfortunately, what's S.O.P. for GE turned out to be almost fatal to the peacock. The difference between Tinker's leadership and GE-style management is almost a casebook study on the differences between bold entrepreneurship and timid management.

In recent years, the networks have lost viewers to more aggressive independent TV stations, cable TV and video cassettes, and so ad revenues are flat, or down. Wright believed that if revenues didn't grow, and moderate inflation continued, along with such built-in cost increases as contractually binding salary increases, obviously the network's profits would begin to decline.

He told the *New York Times*, "From my standpoint, we have no choice but to look at the same future ABC and CBS are looking at. In the next eighteen to twenty-four months, without advertising growth and only moderate inflation, we will not be able to do any better than we've done. Our organization has to understand that in order to have a successful business in five years."

Wrong, Mr. Wright. First, it was Tinker's insistence on seeing a different future than ABC and CBS saw which led to NBC's renaissance, and the simultaneous declines of ABC and CBS. Second, a successful network, like any other business, is only as successful as its product. A TV network's only product is programs, and at NBC, according to one executive, of the 2,000 West Coast employees less than fifty were directly involved in the creation and development of programs. In this light, an across-the-board reduction of five percent seemed not merely foolish, but blind. If anything, the programming division should have been encouraged to increase its budget by at least five percent.

Faced with disastrous ratings and pitiful revenues when he took over, Tinker became the very model of an entrepreneur. First, he understood that the principal capital now is human capital, and encouraged the most creative people in the business to come to NBC with their ideas. Second, he understood that the key to generating wealth is innovation, and, working with NBC's chief programmer, Brandon Tartikoff, he brought us a new kind of TV—a cop show without car chases, another cop show in which the look and the sound are as vital as guns and bad guys, and comedies about an alcoholic bartender, four over-the-hill ladies, and a black middle class family.

"Hill Street Blues," "Miami Vice," "Cheers," "Golden Girls" and "The Cosby Show," along with such other NBC innovations as "St. Elsewhere," in which the doctors and nurses were as vulnerable as their patients, and "L.A. Law," in which the lawyers were as beset as their clients, became contemporary TV—beautifully crafted and performed, sophisticated, innovative, and sometimes controversial.

With the exception of "The Cosby Show," none of these models of TV excellence was an instant hit, but Tinker and Tartikoff stuck by them, in the best entrepreneurial fashion. Tinker didn't follow the audience, he led it and remade it, along with network television itself.

Conversely, though faced with winning ratings and soaring revenues when he took over, Wright became the very model of a dutiful manager, never looking beyond the bottom line, more concerned with cutting costs than improving the product, eschewing innovation, and, above all, ranking careful management over creative entrepreneurship. The moment that he took over, Wright abandoned his predecessor's daring entrepreneurial approach, choosing instead the posture of the reflexive manager, and thus seemed bent on turning the leader into a follower. ABC and CBS were cutting back, so NBC must cut back, too.

In defense of this odd tack, which might be described as following the losers, Wright said, "GE and Bob Wright will have failed if we wait until NBC stumbles and then try to fix it." But, of course, the way to keep NBC on top was to continue developing innovative programming, to move forward, not cut back. Instead of managing NBC's money, Wright should have encouraged its talented programmers and the pool of creative producers, writers and performers drawn to NBC by Tinker and Tartikoff.

Wright said, "Cost and profitability are not necessarily related. You can't guarantee ways to get market share and you can't guarantee ways to keep it. The business is governed by intangibles: viewer tastes, competition, affiliate relations. There is a lack of clarity about where you're going."

In fact, Tinker knew exactly where he was going. He knew that if NBC gave the audience programs that were genuinely new and different, as well as being beautifully crafted, it would not only attract but hold the audience's attention.

If NBC acquired a "lack of clarity" about its direction, it was triggered by Wright himself. In addition to laying off 150 people, heading another 150 toward early retirement following NBC's best year ever, and asking division heads to come up with the five percent budget cuts, he also scolded administrators for overly cautious "belt and suspenders" management (though he was the archetypal belt and suspenders man himself), and suggested that NBC start a political action committee funded with employee contributions.

It seemed that GE-man Wright was determined to turn out the lights at NBC. But, of course, he was playing to an audience of one, his boss, Jack Welch, whom he wanted to succeed. However, it's worth noting that only two NBC chiefs have ever left the post voluntarily. One was Robert Sarnoff, son of the company's founder. The other was Tinker.

One Wall Street analyst said appreciatively of Wright, "He's trying to bring the real world into focus at NBC."

What neither Wright nor the analyst understood is that Tinker was the one who brought the "real world" to NBC when he determined that if he brought the best creative people to the network, and gave them the time, money and leeway to do their best, then the network would thrive. He was right. Network profits increased tenfold during his tenure, TV programming was revolutionized, and NBC's hit shows won critical acclaim and countless Emmys, along with ratings.

Admittedly, Tinker was a tough act to follow, but it was the only act that works in the real world. Entrepreneurs like Tinker know that human capital is the only capital that really counts now. Managers, like Wright, who have spent their corporate lives watching the bottom line, still haven't got the message.

It has been American big business's obsession with the bottom line in the last decade and its continuing inability to see that its workers are its primary asset that has got it into such trouble. Until the Tinkers outnumber the Wrights, America is destined to continue to lag, in vital ways, in the volatile world market.

### *Coda*

Ah, well, history: Mr. Wright looks a lot better. You can call him Mr. Right now. Jack Welch can take credit for the turn-around and for his taste in people, which turned out to be better than mine.

# 9

# LEADERSHIP FOR TOMORROW

*Today's leaders have a very challenging and rewarding role, given the
variety of stakeholder needs they must take into account.*

One of my favorite quotes is by E. B. White, who once said,
"I wake up every morning determined both to change the
world and have one hell of a good time. Sometimes this makes
planning the day a little difficult."

Every leader today shares a similar wake-up call and charge:
both to change the world and have a good time doing it. But
I would add an important footnote: The noble mission of the
leader can't be used to justify the means. In the leadership
arena, character counts.

I'm not saying this casually. My convictions about charac-
ter-based leadership come from years of studies, observations,
and interviews with leaders, and with the people near them—
their direct reports and board members.

In 1980 I decided that I would go out and talk to lots of
people in leadership positions and find out more about what
goes on up close, not through survey research, but through in-
depth interviews and observations, spending time with the
company and getting to know the culture. I interviewed about
150 executives, a variety of leaders from Fortune 500 corporations to employee-owned businesses and entrepreneurial
companies. And in the public sector, I talked with politicians,
mayors, university presidents, museum directors—the widest
variety of people you can imagine. I guess you could say that

my work has been like that of a reporter. I've been listening to people, letting the data pour over me, taking it all in, and then trying to make some sense of what I hear and see.

I was most interested in what the similarities were. I had the hubris to believe that if I could study several exemplary leaders, I could identify a few qualities, characteristics, or competencies that all effective leaders manifest. I was inspired by the first line of one of the great novels, *Anna Karenina*: "All happy families are alike. All unhappy families are peculiar in their own ways." I was interested to see if all successful leaders were alike. I was looking for similarities.

To be sure, there are many superficial and immediately observable differences in leaders. They come in all styles and forms and heights and capacities. Some are articulate and charismatic; others are not. But I had my eye on what it was that distinguished leaders.

### Two Propositions

Two propositions have guided my thinking and my work.

First, I think leadership is character. Character is a word that comes from the Greek "engraved." It's from the French "inscribed." It isn't just a superficial style. It's got to do with who we are as human beings, and what shaped us. I also believe that character is a continuously evolving thing. Unlike some of the Freudians, I don't think it stops at six, I think we continue to acquire and to grow and to develop.

The corollary of this is that the process of becoming a leader, to me, is much the same process as becoming an integrated human being. So I see a real connection between what it takes to be a leader and the process. In fact, if the book *On Becoming a Person* by Carl Rogers hadn't been entitled that before I wrote mine called *On Becoming a Leader*, I thought I could have used that as well.

When you look at the typical criteria that most organizations use to evaluate their executives and managers, there usually are seven: technical competence or business literacy, knowing the territory; people skills, the capacity to bring out and motivate people; conceptual skills, putting things together; results, track record; taste, the capacity to choose terrific people most of the time; judgment, the ability to make wise decisions in a fog of reality and uncertainty; and character, the integrity to walk the talk.

Now, what's interesting about the last two, judgment and character, is that they're the most difficult. We don't know how to teach them. We know they're learned, but it's a challenge to know how they're formed. I've never seen a person derailed because of a lack of technical competence. But I've seen lots of people derailed from positions because of a lack of judgment and character.

Second, to keep their organizations competitive, leaders must create a social architecture capable of generating intellectual capital. What matters most about the structure, architecture, or design of the organization is whether it exemplifies the five Fs: fast, focused, flexible, friendly, and fun. Almost any design will work if the people want it to work. So I'm less concerned about structure than I am about what leaders are doing to motivate people. I think it's ideas, innovation, and quality of the workforce that make all the difference in the world. And the brightest leaders are aware of that.

What matters in most new organizations is the intellectual capital, the brainpower. The frustrating thing is that it's hard to measure. Recently the *New York Times* ran a rhapsodic front-page Sunday business section article about the IBM takeover of Lotus—a $3.5 billion acquisition. One paragraph in particular interested me: "Perhaps the most striking aspect of IBM's takeover bid, and the one that says the most about these times, is that it defies the accepted wisdom on the difficulties of trying to acquire a company whose primary value isn't in its machinery or real estate, but rather in that most mercurial of assets—people."

See, IBM is really buying brains. They're buying terrific people. And when I go around and talk to executives from big and small companies, they say, "My biggest challenge is: How do I release the brainpower?"

So those are my two leadership propositions. And that's why leadership is a very personal thing. Certain leaders are more capable of generating intellectual capital than others. To put it simply, whips and chains no longer work. We've got to think carefully about the qualities that make leaders effective as we move into the next century.

*Four Things People Want*

What do people want from their leaders? I have identified four characteristics that stand out and have deep relevance for tomorrow's corporations.

What most constituents want from their leaders are: 1) purpose, direction, or meaning; 2) trust; 3) a sense of we-can-do-it optimism; and 4) results.

• **Purpose.** I can't exaggerate the significance of a strong determination to achieve a goal—a conviction, a passion, even a skewed distortion of reality that focuses on a particular point of view. And the leader has to express that in various ways. There can be many different purposes. For example, Michael Eisner once said to me, "You know, at Disney, we really don't have a vision statement. We have a strong point of view here about what Disney's culture is like." And he said, "We also like to bring in people with a strong point of view. It's uncanny. Every Friday, when we have our presidents' meeting where we're making million-dollar decisions on what should be our next animated feature, I've never seen it fail that the person with the strongest point of view almost always wins the argument." I thought that was an interesting statement.

Max DePree, the now-retired chariman of Herman Miller, said, "The first task of a leader is to help define reality." That's another way of talking about purpose. Without a sense of alignment behind that purpose, the company will be in trouble because the opposite of having purpose is drifting aimlessly. And it can't be any old purpose that will galvanize and energize and enthrall people. It has to have meaning and resonance.

My favorite way of talking about meaning, and it's certainly true when we look at resumes, is a marvelous Peanuts cartoon featuring Lucy and Schroeder. Lucy's looking at Schroeder rather wistfully, and Schroeder's playing the piano. Lucy asks Schroeder if he knows what love is. And Schroeder immediately stands at attention and says, "Love. Noun. An attraction to or affiliation with a person or persons." And he sits down and starts playing the piano again. Lucy looks reproachfully and says, "On paper, he's great." All the mission statements in the world suffer from that same thing.

• **Trust.** Leaders generate and sustain trust. I needn't tell you how difficult that is today. We live in a world of temps, of not having the same compact we used to have. The kid growing up in the Depression era figured, "Well, I'll be successful if I just work hard, put one foot ahead of the next, get a job and hold it." That's not the case today. The trust factor is the social glue that keeps any act together. Without it, it's easy to lose and very hard to gain.

To trust other people, to have confidence in them, we need to see evidence of competence. I once interviewed Hollywood producer and director Sydney Pollack. He's so highly respected and has such confidence in directing that he could get almost anybody to work with him on a movie. He never makes anybody feel wrong. We expect our leaders to be competent.

Another aspect of trust is openness. I can't overemphasize the importance of encouraging openness, even dissent.

I once received a letter from an executive who wrote: "We've got thousands of folks, union workers, who want the world to be the way it used to be, and they are very unwilling to accept any alternative forecast of the future." The problem is that there's no trust in that organization. This executive was an old-fashioned, control-and-command type who never could regenerate the trust among the key stakeholders. The union members were not the problem in this case.

One of the best ways to build trust is by deep listening. It's the most powerful dynamic of human interaction when people feel they're being heard. Listening doesn't mean agreeing, but it does mean having the empathic reach to understand another.

• **Optimism.** Almost all executives believe that they can achieve their goals and have a happy outcome. This is what I would call a distorted perception of reality. I was taught in graduate school to think that one criterion of mental health was an accurate perception of reality. But I sense that many leaders perceive that they can really change the world.

Almost all leaders are purveyors of hope. Their optimism fascinates me because it is so pervasive and so powerful. I don't think it can be built on phoney grounds either.

A marvelous story about Reagan comes from Richard Wirthlin, who for seven years was Reagan's pollster. One of Reagan's strengths was how he could convey that sense of optimism to the public, which at times was very badly needed.

Wirthlin said that in 1982, when we were still in an economic recession, Reagan's approval rating dropped to 32 percent, the lowest on record for any President in the second year of office. A few months earlier, shortly after the attempted assassination, his approval rating was off the charts—up in the low 90s.

When Wirthlin visited the Oval Office, Reagan said, "Tell me the news," and Wirthlin said, "Not good." And Reagan said, "What do you mean?" and Wirthlin said, "32 percent—it's the worst it's been for any President in his second year in office." Reagan smiled and said, "Dick, stop worrying. I'll just try to go out there and get shot again."

• **Action and results.** The last quality common to leaders is a bias toward action. That is, the capacity to convert purpose and vision into action. It just isn't enough to have the great vision you can trust. It's got to be manifest in some external products and results. Most leaders are pragmatic dreamers or practical idealists, if that's not too much of an oxymoron. They step up and take their shots every day, perhaps knowing what hockey player and philosopher Wayne Gretsky once said, "You miss 100 percent of the shots you don't take."

Those are the things that stand out as I talk to people. And I think these are the things people look for when they vote for political candidates. Certainly, the trust issue will continue to be a main issue of every campaign.

# 10

## DEVELOPING LEADERS

*In an organization, it is everybody's
responsibility to develop leaders.*

Because we learn mainly through observation, we look to
see what the definition of success or failure is around the organization. Being acute observers, we try to model ourselves
after those definitions. So, how do organizations develop their
leaders? They do it all the time, usually unconsciously, regardless of their specific leader identification and who the hot people are and how they push them through the organization.
Everyday, people are learning all the good and all the bad
lessons, whether the organization knows it or not. Every waking minute, people are observing.

Here are some simple guidelines for developing leaders:

• First, identify those individuals who grow leaders. Many
people are simply terrific at giving birth to leaders. They're
good coaches. Identify them and then reward them. When I
chaired the search committee for our new president at the
University of Southern California, we looked for a person
with more people who had worked under him who went on to
become university presidents. But rarely are these people
rewarded. So find out who the good coaches are and then
reward them.

• Make sure the organization identifies what the developmental experiences are. What are those things that actually
produce good leaders? For example, one recipe for developing

leadership is to appoint a person to head up an important task force, within a certain time frame, with a highly significant, not peripheral, problem, but one that is salient and important to the company, under top management scrutiny, where that individual has, in the task force, members of different parts of the organization.

The companies I know that are good at growing leaders really believe in cross-functional experience. For example, there's not a person at ARCO, to take one company, that does a good job, or Glaxo, a huge pharmaceutical company, or Johnson & Johnson, who doesn't have to work in every single function of the business. They really have to develop business literacy. They have to be in planning, in staffing, in computers, in legal and research. They have to experience and taste and be subculture hoppers. They have to be all around the place before they get to the top.

• The more bosses you work under, the better. The more the merrier because people learn as much from bad bosses as they do from good ones. They learn most from bosses with extreme talents of both an ogreish kind or a terrific kind. Organizations should develop a menu of developmental experiences and determine at what stages in a career certain developmental experiences would be more promising. For example, for new employees, challenging first jobs would be terribly important, but usually they're put into boring jobs. I would think that in midcareer another set of developmental experiences would be necessary (such as an advanced management program at some university). And at senior career, yet another set of developmental experiences.

• Encourage managers to surrender the people who are terrific in their jobs and permit broadening experiences for them. Mentoring would also be a part of this. Mentoring should be a formal system, not simply a let-it-happen accident.

For example, in the Persian Gulf war, General Norman Schwarzkopf, a veteran of the Vietnam War, made one thing extremely clear: To have any successful leadership, you have to have a clear mission or vision and a clear-cut target. The idea of a vision or mission, and managing that mission or vision, is terribly important in wars and in organizations.

An effective leader doesn't necessarily say, "I want to be a leader." Most of the not-for-profit or "movement" leaders I've talked with—Gloria Steinem, Betty Friedan, and the others—didn't start out saying, "I want a position of power." I think they wanted to influence through voice, or they were able to see a problem and identify a solution. Kathleen Brown, the daughter of former California Governor Pat Brown and the sister of Governor Jerry Brown, said something very interesting. She said the difference between men and women, as she put it, is that women seek power in order to address issues, while men address issues in order to seek power. It's an interesting distinction. Most of the people I got to know in my interviews were people who wanted to express themselves—their essence—rather than to prove themselves.

Leaders of companies must have a long-range perspective, hard as that is to achieve given the Wall Street climate. Honestly, when I look at successful organizations, they almost all have a long-range perspective. There may be some downturns, but basically I think that's a critical necessity. Ironically, when Nicholas Brady took over as secretary of the Treasury, he said his major, long-term goal was to try to shift American industries from a short-range to a long-range perspective. It still hasn't happened.

There are two things I'm clear about when I think about organizations today: 1) the organizations that will succeed in the white-knuckle decade of the '90s are those that take seriously, and sustain through action, their belief that their competitive advantage is their people and their development; and 2) post-bureaucratic organizations will require leadership that is more interactional, that encourages healthy conflict, that is more concerned with cross-functional education and training, that rewards people who are good coaches, and that promotes people who listen to the ideas of others, who abandon their own egos to the talents of others. All of these things are going to make for a new form of leadership in a post-bureaucratic world. If all that happens, then this country might have a chance.

# 11

## FOUR COMPETENCIES
## OF GREAT LEADERS

*Successful leaders share some things in common, and among these are the astute management of attention, meaning, trust, and self.*

As I researched the book *Leaders*, I traveled around the country spending time with ninety of the most successful leaders in the nation, sixty from corporations and thirty from the public sector.

The group of sixty corporate leaders was not especially different from any profile of top leadership in America. The median age was fifty-six. Most were white males, with six black men and six women in the group. The only surprising finding was that all the CEOs not only were married to their first spouse, but also seemed enthusiastic about the institution of marriage. Examples of the CEOs are Bill Kieschnick, chairman and CEO of ARCO, and the late Ray Kroc of McDonald's restaurants.

Public-sector leaders included Harold Williams, who then chaired the SEC; Neil Armstrong, a genuine all-American hero who happened to be at the University of Cincinnati; three elected officials; two orchestra conductors; and two winning athletics coaches.

If I have learned anything from my research, it is this: The factor that empowers the workforce and ultimately determines which organizations succeed or fail is the leadership of those organizations. When strategies, processes, or cultures change, the key to improvement remains leadership.

Leaders are people who do the right thing; managers are people who do things right. Both roles are crucial, and they differ profoundly. I often observe people in top positions doing the wrong thing well.

Given my definition, one of the key problems facing American organizations is that they are under-led and over-managed. They do not pay enough attention to doing the right thing, while they pay too much attention to doing things right. Part of the fault lies with our schools of management; we teach people how to be good technicians and good staff people, but we don't train people for leadership.

My first goal was to find people with leadership ability, in contrast to just "good managers"—true leaders who affect the culture, who are the social architects of their organizations, and who create and maintain values.

My second goal was to find these leaders' common traits, a task that has required much more probing than I expected. For a while, I sensed much more diversity than commonality among them. The group comprises both left-brain and right-brain thinkers; some who dress for success and some who don't; well-spoken, articulate leaders and laconic, inarticulate ones; some John Wayne types, and some who are definitely the opposite. Interestingly, the group includes only a few stereotypically charismatic leaders.

Despite the diversity, I identified four areas of competence shared by all ninety: the management of attention, meaning, trust, and self.

### 1. Management of Attention

One of the traits most apparent in these leaders is their ability to draw others to them, not because they have a vision, a dream, a set of intentions, an agenda, a frame of reference, but because they communicate an extraordinary focus of commitment which attracts people to them. One of the leaders was described as making people want to join him; he enrolls them in his vision.

Leaders, then, manage attention through a compelling vision that brings others to a place they have not been before. I came to this understanding in a roundabout way, as this anecdote illustrates.

One of the people I most wanted to interview was one of the few I couldn't seem to reach. He refused to answer my letters or phone calls. I even tried getting in touch with the members of his board. He is Leon Fleischer, a well-known child prodigy who grew up to become a prominent pianist, conductor, and musicologist. What I did not know about him was that he had lost the use of his right hand and no longer performed.

When I called him originally to recruit him for the University of Cincinnati faculty, he declined and told me he was working with orthopedic specialists to regain the use of his hand. He did visit the campus, and I was impressed with his commitment to staying in Baltimore, near the medical institution where he received therapy.

Fleischer was the only person who kept turning me down for an interview, and finally I gave up. A couple of summers later I was in Aspen, Colorado, while Fleischer was conducting the Aspen Music Festival. I tried to reach him again, even leaving a note on his dressing room door, but I got no answer.

One day in downtown Aspen, I saw two perspiring young cellists carrying their instruments and offered them a ride to the music tent. They hopped in the back of my Jeep, and, as we rode, I questioned them about Fleischer.

"I'll tell you why he is so great," said one. "He doesn't waste our time."

Fleischer finally agreed not only to be interviewed, but to let me watch him rehearse and conduct music classes. I linked the way I saw him work with that simple sentence, "He doesn't waste our time." Every moment Fleischer was before the orchestra, he knew exactly what sound he wanted. He didn't waste time because his intentions were always evident. What united him with the other musicians was their concern with intention and outcome.

When I reflected on my own experience, it struck me that when I was most effective, it was because I knew what I wanted. When I was ineffective, it was because I was unclear about my desired outcome.

So, the first leadership competency is the management of attention through a set of intentions or a vision, not in a mystical or religious sense, but in the sense of outcome, goal, or direction.

## 2. Management of Meaning

To make dreams apparent to others, and to align people with them, leaders must communicate their vision. Communication and alignment work together. Leaders make ideas tangible and real to others, so they can support them. For no matter how marvelous the vision, the effective leader must use a metaphor, a word, or a model to make that vision clear to others.

The leader's goal is not mere explanation or clarification, but the creation of meaning. My favorite baseball joke is exemplary: In the ninth inning of a key playoff game, with a 3 and 2 count on the batter, the umpire hesitates a split second in calling the pitch. The batter whirls around angrily and says, "Well, what is it?" The umpire barks back, "It ain't nothing until I call it!"

The more far-flung and complex the organization, the more critical this ability is. Effective leaders can communicate ideas through several organizational layers, across great distances, even through the jamming signals of special interest groups and opponents.

When I was a university president, a group of administrators and I would hatch what we knew was a great idea. Then we would do the right thing: delegate, delegate, delegate. But when the product or policy finally appeared, it scarcely resembled our original idea.

This process occurred so often that I gave it a name: the Pinocchio effect. (I am sure Geppetto had no idea how Pinocchio would look when he finished carving him.) The Pinocchio effect leaves us surprised. Because of inadequate communication, results rarely resemble our expectations.

We read and hear so much about information that we tend to overlook the importance of meaning. Actually, the more bombarded a society or organization, the more deluged with facts and images, the greater its thirst for meaning. Leaders integrate facts, concepts, and anecdotes into meaning for the public.

Not all the leaders in my group are word masters. They get people to understand and support their goals in a variety of ways.

The ability to manage attention and meaning comes from the whole person. It is not enough to use the right buzzword or a cute technique, or to hire a public relations person to write speeches.

Consider, instead, Frank Dale, former publisher of the now defunct Los Angeles afternoon newspaper, the *Herald Examiner*. Dale's charge was to cut into the market share of his morning competitor, the *Los Angeles Times*. When he first joined the newspaper he created a campaign with posters picturing the *Herald Examiner* behind and slightly above the *Times*. The whole campaign was based on this potent message of how the *Herald Examiner* would overtake the *Times*.

I interviewed Dale at his office, and when he sat down at his desk and fastened around him a safety belt like those on airplanes, I couldn't suppress a smile. He did this to remind me and everybody else of the risks the newspaper entailed. His whole person contributed to the message.

No one is more cynical than a newspaper reporter. You can imagine the reactions that traveled the halls of the *Herald Examiner* building. At the same time, nobody forgot what Frank Dale was trying to communicate. And that is the management of meaning.

### 3. Management of Trust

Trust is essential to all organizations. The main determinant of trust is reliability, what I call constancy. When I talked to the board members or staffs of these leaders, I heard certain phrases again and again: "She is all of a piece." "Whether you like it or not, you always know where he is coming from, what he stands for."

When John Paul II visited this country, he gave a press conference. One reporter asked how the Pope could account for allocating funds to build a swimming pool at the papal summer palace. He responded quickly: "I like to swim. Next question." He did not rationalize about medical reasons or claim he got the money from a special source.

A recent study showed people would much rather follow individuals they can count on, even when they disagree with their viewpoint, than people they agree with but who shift positions frequently. I cannot emphasize enough the significance of constancy and focus.

Margaret Thatcher's re-election in Great Britain is another excellent example. When she won office in 1979, observers predicted she would quickly revert to defunct Labor Party policies.

She did not. In fact, a *London Times* article appeared with the headline (parodying Christopher Fry's play), "The Lady's Not for Returning." She did not return to the old policies; instead, she remained constant, focused, and all of a piece.

### 4. Management of Self

The fourth leadership competency is management of self, knowing one's skills, and deploying them effectively. Management of self is critical; without it, leaders and managers can do more harm than good. Like incompetent doctors, incompetent managers can make life worse, make people sicker and less vital. (The term "iatrogenic", by the way, refers to illness caused by doctors and hospitals.) Some managers give themselves heart attacks and nervous breakdowns; still worse, many are "carriers," causing their employees to be ill.

Leaders know themselves; they know their strengths and nurture them.

The leaders in my group seemed unacquainted with the concept of failure. What you or I might call a failure, they referred to as a mistake. I began collecting synonyms for the word *failure* mentioned in the interviews, and I found more than 20: mistake, error, false start, bloop, flop, loss, miss, foul-up, stumble, botch, bungle . . . but not failure.

One CEO told me that if she had a knack for leadership, it was the capacity to make as many mistakes as she could as soon as possible, and thus get them out of the way. Another said that a mistake is simply "another way of doing things." These leaders learn from and use something that doesn't go well; it is not a failure, but simply the next step.

When I asked Harold Williams, president of the Getty Foundation, to name the experience that most shaped him as a leader he said it was being passed over for the presidency of Norton Simon. When it happened, he was furious and demanded reasons, most of which he considered idiotic. Finally, a friend told him that some of the reasons were valid and he should change. He did, and about a year and a half later became president.

Or consider coach Ray Meyer of DePaul University, whose team finally lost at home after winning twenty-nine straight home games. I called him to ask how he felt. He said, "Great.

Now we can start concentrating on winning, not on not losing."

Consider Broadway producer Harold Prince, who calls a press conference the morning after his show opens, before reading the reviews, to announce his next play. Or suffragist Susan B. Anthony, who said, "Failure is impossible." Or Fletcher Byrum, who after 22 years as president of Coopers, was asked about his hardest decision. He replied that he did not know what a hard decision was; that whenever worried, he accepted the possibility of being wrong. Byrum said that worry was an obstacle to clear thinking.

### *Empowerment: The Effect of Leadership*

Leadership can be felt throughout an organization. It gives pace and energy to the work and empowers the workforce. Empowerment is the collective effect of leadership. In organizations with effective leaders, empowerment is most evident in four themes:

• **People feel significant.** Everyone feels that he or she makes a difference to the success of the organization.

• **Learning and competence matter.** Leaders value learning and mastery, and so do people who work for leaders.

• **People are part of a community.** Where there is leadership, there is a team, a family, a unity.

• **Work is exciting.** Where there are leaders, work is stimulating, challenging, fascinating, and fun.

The following two paragraphs were taken from a personal conversation with David Berltew. His words elegantly sum up the essence of this chapter.

> *I believe the lack of two concepts in modern organization life is largely responsible for the alienation and lack of meaning so many experience in their work.*
>
> *One of these is the concept of quality. Modern industrial society has been oriented to quantity, providing more goods and services for everyone. Quantity is measured in money; we are a money-oriented society. Quality often is not measured at all, but is appreciated intuitively. Our response to quality is a feeling. Feelings of quality are connected intimately with our experience of meaning, beauty, and value in our lives.*

*Closely linked to that concept of quality is that of dedication, even love, of our work. This dedication is evoked by quality and is the force that energizes high-performing systems. When we love our work, we need not be managed by hopes of reward or fears of punishment. We can create systems that facilitate our work, rather than being preoccupied with checks and controls of people who want to beat or exploit the system.*

# 12

## TEN TRAITS OF
## DYNAMIC LEADERS

*Dynamic leaders possess some distinguishing personality traits
that give them the power and passion to succeed.*

When Burt Nanus and I interviewed top executives and
gifted entrepreneurs who make things happen in America, our
study identified four main competencies common to all leaders: the management of attention, meaning, trust and self.
Here, I attempt to extract some common personality traits.

**1. Self-knowledge.** There is no greater teacher than
responsibility—especially at an early age. With responsibility
and accountability, you gain self-insight through some hall of
mirrors, some prismatic way of seeing yourself in a variety of
circumstances.

Each of the ninety people we studied in connection with
our book, *Leaders*, seemed to have a great deal of self-knowledge, especially knowledge of what their talents were and how
to best deploy them. How they arrived at this knowledge varied enormously. But let me cite one example. When I did
some work with Chase Manhattan, I discovered that many of
their top executives had served in some strange and exotic,
typically foreign, assignment. Most had spent a hitch in an
overseas post.

I think there's something positive to say about being
upended, about having all your assumptions and beliefs questioned, about finding yourself a stranger in a strange land.
The situation creates a great deal of self-knowledge. You learn

a lot not only about another culture, but also about your own culture and about yourself.

Now, the situation doesn't have to be in an exotic land. I think of "foreign land" more as a metaphor. There are several positions and places within most corporations that could serve the same purpose, that would be a sort of strange upending, a reframing, a kick in the shins, so to speak—an experience that would make people think about who and what they are.

**2. Open to feedback.** Effective leaders develop valued and varied sources of feedback on their behavior and performance. And one of the best sources for many executives is a spouse. Of the forty executives of Fortune 200 companies in our study, all but two were still married to their first spouse and very enthusiastic about the whole institution of marriage.

Again, there's something to say about a lasting relationship with someone you trust totally, someone who provides you with reflective back talk. There's something to say about finding any valued source of feedback. The trick is getting the best feedback possible, being open to it, and changing for the better because of it.

**3. Eager to learn and improve.** I find that effective leaders are great askers and listeners. When it has to do with their work, their job, their company, they're wide awake. They know what they are good at doing, and they nurture and develop those skills and talents extraordinarily. They want to get better. In some cases, they are more eager to learn and more open than I would have thought possible.

Almost all leaders have a bias toward change, and they learn from experience that you can't get positive change unless you're open to feedback and look around as you walk through life. Also, they're open to new information because they don't want to be blindsided, to get hit by something they don't see coming. They are extraordinarily thirsty for new knowledge.

**4. Curious, risk takers.** Most leaders are adventurous, risk takers, curious—amazingly curious. They seem to walk through life with their eyebrows raised. And they seem to be capable of taking great risks—always getting involved in situations that they did not realize until later were dangerous.

One individual described himself as a Donald Duck, walking through mine fields which were going off behind him, out of hearing almost, never quite realizing what he was getting himself into. Another individual, Norman Lear, quoted Longfellow, comparing life to a journey. And he talked about the significance not of getting there, but of the journey itself.

I'll bet that these leaders are going to live a long time because of their curiosity, their unending fascination with new thoughts and ideas. That's part of what makes these people spectacular.

**5. Concentrate at work.** Of the people we studied, one individual founded, owned, and managed a very large company. In spite of his achievement, he first struck me as flat, insipid, inarticulate. But when I got to know him better, I noticed an irresistible persistence about him. You wouldn't pick up on it in ordinary conversation or by just knowing him socially. Because of that persistence, he was very effective as a leader; in fact, he surprised me a great deal, as did others who were not graceful and comfortable in their interpersonal relations. It wasn't until I got to know them on the "shop floor," got to watch them work, that I could see their concentration at work. It was a degree of concentration I would not have predicted. And that was probably because they really had a skewed vision about life, which also informed their genius.

These are people who have very few interpersonal skills, but have a concentration that is almost alarming—their caliper eyes focused primarily on their work, on the company, on the goals, on the mission. Offhand, I wouldn't have expected them to be that effective. But they were extraordinarily effective with their people and within their worlds.

**6. Learn from adversity.** Almost invariably, great leaders have had a significant setback, crisis or failure in their lives. Many of the leaders I studied faced adversity early in their lives. Four of them had chronic illnesses. Three others were raised as orphans.

One man, John Wooden, the legendary coach of UCLA, was grateful that he had opportunities to fail early in life because the crucial criteria for him was not that he had failed before, but that failure helped prepare him for future success. The actual phrase he used was "fitness for social action." His concern was to prepare his team for future events. The aim was not simply having a good season or winning several games in a row or even being national champions. Rather what mattered, in his mind, was that his players learn from both failure and success, that they acquire a preparation, a fitness for future action, which he thinks is a major characteristic of successful teams.

**7. Balance tradition and change.** Effective executives learn to balance tradition with change. That, for me, was a particularly hard lesson to learn. When I served as president of the University of Cincinnati (1971 to 1977), I often moved too quickly in what was known to be a very conservative, proud, and traditional climate. Not immersing myself sufficiently in the history of both the university and the city led to a great many mistakes on my part. I didn't do a thorough enough diagnosis of the culture.

Alfred North Whitehead once said that to be an effective leader you've got to adhere both to traditions as well as the need for revision and change. I was much too focused on revision and change. I did not adhere enough to the principles of tradition and stability. This got me into an enormous amount of trouble.

On the other hand, I wouldn't have done some things that turned out to be extremely successful if I had been too bound by the history and culture. So there's a paradox here. You've got to be aware of traditions, but not get entrapped by them.

**8. Open style.** As a university president, I had a very open style, as open as possible. I really wanted to set up my office as a mini-university, a place where we all could learn.

I even tried to do what coaches do: to review a major event to learn from all the mistakes and the successes. The idea was to be extremely reflective about what we, as an administrative team, were doing, even if it meant making myself and others open and vulnerable to criticism.

One day each week, from 3 p.m. on, I opened the office to anyone on campus. No appointment necessary—just come on in. On some afternoons, we had as many as thirty people at a time in my office, sitting around and hearing me respond directly to questions from a variety of constituents and stakeholders—faculty, staff, alumni, parents—sometimes until 10 p.m.! It became an open forum to educate everyone about what was going on in the university. I finally began asking all the senior vice presidents to sit in on these sessions. I realized these would be the people making the changes.

**9. Work well with systems.** Every leader soon realizes that he or she can't handle every problem, that he or she can't handle all things one-on-one, that he or she has to rely heavily on staff and work with systems if things are going to get better.

I used to think I could handle almost anything on an interpersonal level. But I learned that I couldn't deal with everything directly without undercutting my people. If I had a problem within the school of medicine, for example, I could not resolve that problem directly and still maintain the dignity and influence of the dean's office. So, therefore, I had a rule: communication but not decision.

Another benefit of the open forum was that people began to see that the president wasn't the only person doing something. Some people see the president as a man on a white horse, a charismatic figure who is going to solve all of their problems. Once involved in an open forum, they began to see the systemic aspects of all the decisions.

**10. Serve as models and mentors.** Many leaders take great pride in serving as models and mentors. In fact, from my days as a university president, I take the most pride from the fact that ten of my associates—two women and eight men—later became extremely successful university or college presidents, most of them at more prestigious universities than Cincinnati. That to me was a triumph.

And I attribute that triumph to making the entire period a learning process. I was probably overly aware of the very process of being a leader. I would use every experience didactically. I was rolling my own. I was inventing the whole thing as we went along. But all of us, especially the people working directly for me, learned so much about what to do and what not to do.

# 13

## CREATIVE LEADERSHIP

*Leaders create vision, trust, meaning, success, and
healthy environments—if they survive the bureaucracy.*

Leadership is all about innovating and initiating.
Management is about copying and managing the status quo.
Leadership is creative, adaptive, and agile. Leadership looks at
the horizon, not just at the bottom line. A leader does the
right things, which implies a goal, a direction, an objective, a
vision, a dream, a path, a reach.

Joseph Campbell notes that lots of people spend their lives
climbing a ladder—and then they get to the top of the wrong
wall. Most losing organizations are over-managed and under-
led. Their managers accomplish the wrong things beautifully
and efficiently. They climb the wrong wall.

Managing is about efficiency. Leading is about effectiveness. Managing is about how. Leading is about what and why.
Management is about systems, controls, procedures, policies,
structure. Leadership is about trust—about people.

### Six Things a Leader Creates
Leadership is a creative enterprise, and among the many
things a leader creates are the following six.

**1. A leader creates a compelling vision.** If you want to
lead people, first get them to buy into a shared vision and
then translate that vision into action. Leaders take people to
a new place—and leaders draw other people to them by

enrolling them in their vision. Leaders inspire and empower people; they pull, rather than push. This "pull" style attracts and energizes people to enroll in the vision and motivates people by bringing them to identify with the task and the goal, rather than by rewarding or punishing them. I mentioned this once in a lecture at AT&T, and a woman in the audience said, "I have a deaf daughter, so I've learned American Sign Language. This is the sign for manage." She held out her hands as if she were holding onto the reins of a horse, or restraining something. And she went on, "This is the ASL sign for lead." She cradled her arms and rocked them back and forth the way a parent would nurture a child. I was impressed with that.

**2. A leader creates a climate of trust.** Next, learn how to generate and sustain trust. To do this, reward people for disagreeing, reward innovation, and tolerate failure. Don't fire people because they goof. But remember: A lot of trust comes not from a particular technique, but from the character of the leader. To create trust, you need three things: 1) *Competence.* Followers have to have some trust in the leader's capacity to do the job. One person I interviewed for my book was director Sydney Pollack. One of the reasons people want to work with him is they know he has a track record of Academy Award hits. They know he's competent at what he does. 2) *Congruity.* The leader is a person of integrity. If you're an effective leader, what you say is congruent with what you do, and that's congruent with what you feel, and that's congruent with what your vision is. People would much rather follow individuals they can count on, even when they disagree with their viewpoint, than people they agree with, but who shift positions frequently. 3) *Constancy.* People want a sense that their leader is on their side, that he or she will be constant. Competence, congruity, and constancy—those are qualities a leader must embody to create and sustain trust.

**3. A leader creates meaning.** You start with vision. You build trust. And you create meaning. A leader creates meaning by creating an environment where people are reminded of what's important. The leader helps define the mission of the organization and models the behavior that will move the organization toward those goals. In Eastern Europe, the people who have recently gotten into power all seem to be people who can put words to goals and aspirations. Whether it's a playwright in Czechoslovakia or the journalist who's the prime minister of Poland, or the present prime minister of Romania who's a poet—these are people who can use words beautifully to express the collective goals of their people. That's important. When leaders don't do that, people get disaffected. What creates meaning is primarily the concept, the idea. Words are powerful. Words endowed with relevance and purpose create meaning.

**4. A leader creates success,** often from failure (mistakes). Successful leaders perceive and handle "failure" differently. The word "failure," to most people, connotes something that's terminal and lifeless. But leaders embrace error. They see "failure" as a "mistake," a "glitch," a "hash," a "miscue," a "false start," or a "misdirection."

Most of the people I interviewed looked forward to mistakes because they felt that someone who hadn't made a mistake hadn't been trying hard enough. Television producer Norman Lear told me, "Wherever I trip is where the treasure lies." Katherine Graham, publisher of the *Washington Post*, said, "For me, a mistake is simply another way of doing things."

The leaders I met, whatever walk of life they were from, whatever institution they were presiding over, always referred back to some failure—something that happened to them that was personally difficult, even traumatic, something that made them feel that desperate sense of hitting bottom—as something they thought was almost a necessity. It's as if at that moment the iron entered their soul; that moment created the resilience that leaders need. For instance, there's Mike McGee, the former athletic director at the University of Southern California (and now AD of another USC, the University of South Carolina). The most significant learning experience in his life was when he was fired as head coach at Duke. He learned from it because he figured out what was wrong.

The thing about failure is that it demands explanation. The people who don't succeed are the people who look at failure and don't learn from it. They blame somebody else, they blame the stars, but not themselves. All the successful leaders I've met learned to embrace error and to learn from it. And real leaders keep the message moving; they make it clear to those they lead that there is no failure, only mistakes that give us feedback and tell us what to do next. When people turn away from leaders, sometimes it's because the leaders aren't very good. There's no reason to be attracted to incompetent leadership.

**5. A leader creates a healthy, empowering environment.** We have a basic ambivalence about authority in our society. We enshrine the myth of the lone hero, the outlaw, the renegade, the John Wayne cowboy, Gary Cooper in "High Noon." The celebration of self is deeply embedded in our culture. Our nation was founded by pioneers and by people who were oppressed, and leaders are always suspect. In our recent history, there's been a lot of disappointment with leaders. Indeed, some managers do more harm than good. Think about your own work experience. Have you ever worked for anyone who made you nervous or made you a little nuts needlessly? A lot of stress and burnout have to do with bosses who communicate mixed messages. You're never sure where they're at. Or they're insecure and they make your job impossible.

Effective leadership empowers the workforce. An empowered workforce means one that's committed, that feels its members are learning, that they're competent. They have a sense of human bond, a sense of community, a sense of meaning in their work. Even people who do not especially like each other feel the sense of community. A feeling of significance is so important.

Good leaders make people feel that they're at the very heart of things, not at the periphery. Everyone feels that he or she makes a difference to the success of the organization. When that happens, people feel centered and that gives their work meaning.

Leadership gives the workforce a sense of meaning, of significance, of competence, of community, of commitment rather than compliance. It also gives the workforce a sense of fun. It makes work something you look forward to, something pleasant. You get a kick out of work. Noel Coward once said, "Work should be more fun than fun."

**6. A leader creates flat, flexible, adaptive, decentralized systems and organizations.** Bureaucracies don't create leaders. They create managers, and bureaucrats. They create people who wear square hats, not sombreros. Bureaucracies are self-sustaining only in times of stability, when the environment is placid. They are very ineffective when times are changing. When the world is turbulent, the managerial environment is spastic, fluid, and volatile. Then the bureaucracy seems to be particularly inadequate because it keeps repeating yesterday's lessons and fighting the last war. Bureaucracies tend to suppress real leadership because real leaders disequilibrate systems; they create disorder and instability, even chaos. Real leaders change the very system in which bureaucracies are based.

Healthcare and telecommunications are industries that will be buffeted and vulnerable during this, the "white-knuckle decade." Healthcare has extensive technological pressures, and the pressures of regulation and possible deregulation. Global pressures, pressures with changing demographics, environmental challenges—all of these affect telecommunications and healthcare more than other sectors of the economy.

Companies are being evaluated now according to their ability to operate in the context of a zero-time-lag world. Managing change is going to be the ultimate leadership challenge. We need strong leadership in organizations based on a network or a flattened hierarchy model—a more decentralized model where the key words are acknowledge, create, and empower. Organizations that operate on the model of bureaucracy—based on the words control, order, and predict—are not going to cut it. They already aren't. Almost half (47 percent) of the organizations that were Fortune 500 companies between 1979 and 1989 are no longer there, because they weren't adaptive enough. In this decade, we need more leadership and less bureaucracy. It's either change or die.

### Three Ways to Kill Creative Leadership

In organizations of all types and sizes, we have effectively killed and buried creative leadership in the following ways:

• **Emphasize managing instead of pioneering.** Many U.S. companies are very well managed, but poorly led. Managers may handle routine tasks well, but no one bothers to ask whether "this" should be done at all. Routine work smothers creativity and change, but because routine work is easier to deal with, there's an unconscious conspiracy to immerse ourselves in routine and avoid the tough questions.

• **Insist on harmony and pseudo-agreement.** The cohesiveness of most organizations depends on a commonly held set of values. Anyone who does not share the common culture is an outsider, at angle to the conventional (and often misguided) wisdom. But unanimity leads to stagnation. The individual who sees things differently is the company's vital link to change and adaptation. Every leader, like King Lear, needs at least one fool to challenge what is sacred and to herald the advent of cosmic shifts.

• **Reward destructive achievers.** Our whole attitude toward leaders is tainted by the likes of Gary Hart, Ivan F. Boesky, and Oliver North. They have in common two of the three qualities that every leader needs: ambition and expertise. They lack the third: integrity.

### Three Abilities to Look For

To break through the barriers to strong leadership, companies must look for executives with three rare qualities:

• **Ability to articulate a vision.** Leaders must create a compelling vision that takes people to a new place and then translate that vision into reality. Former Scandinavian Airlines Systems chief executive Jan Carlzon was exemplary in this respect. His vision was to make SAS one of the few air carriers that will still exist in the year 2000. To accomplish this, he developed two goals: to make SAS one percent better than its competitors in 100 different ways and to create a market niche. He chose the business traveler. To attract them, he broke away from the traditional pyramid-shaped organization and created small, autonomous work groups. He put in profit-sharing plans and charged groups with making every single interaction with customers a meaningful "moment of truth."

• **Ability to embrace error.** Failure, error, and mistakes all require explanation. Moreover, the ability to embrace error is an important component in creating an atmosphere in which risk taking is encouraged. As successful film director Sydney Pollack tells his people, the only mistake is to do nothing.

• **Ability to encourage "reflective back talk."** Real leaders know the importance of having someone around who will tell the truth. Lee Iacocca encourages what he calls "contrarians." One of the most intriguing discoveries that I made in my research on chief executives is that almost all were still married to their first spouse. The reason may be that the spouse is the one person they can totally trust. The back talk from the spouse, the trusted one, is reflective because it allows the leader to learn, to find out more about himself or herself. Plato had it right as usual: All learning, he said, is basically a form of recovery and reflection.

### Three Questions to Ask

A leader's effectiveness can be gauged by asking these three questions:

• **Do workers feel significant?** When a leader is truly leading, people feel that what they do has meaning.

• **Is the work felt to be exciting?** Leaders will "pull," not "push" workers toward a goal. They do so by making the work stimulating, challenging, even fun. This "pull" style of influence attracts and energizes people, motivating them to achieve by identification. In the long run, it's far more effective than motivating people through coercion.

• **Does the leader embody the organization's ethics and values?** If the unofficial norms of a corporation differ markedly from either the formal code of ethics or the chief executive's personal behavior, then there's bound to be trouble. Sending mixed messages to employees on ethical issues, more than anything else, is one of the most destructive things a leader can do.

Gandhi once said: "We must be the change we wish to see in the world." The status quo will not help us march ahead—that I can guarantee.

# 14

# LEADERS INVENT THEMSELVES

*We are our own raw material from which we must invent and fashion ourselves as leaders as we go along.*

Leaders come in every size, shape, and disposition—short, tall, neat, sloppy, young, old, male, and female. Nevertheless, they all seem to share some, if not all, of the following five ingredients:

• **Vision.** The first basic ingredient of leadership is a guiding vision. The leader has a clear idea of what he or she wants to do—professionally and personally—and the strength to persist in the face of setbacks, even failures. Unless you know where you're going, and why, you cannot possibly get there.

• **Passion.** The second basic ingredient of leadership is passion—the underlying passion for the promises of life, combined with a very particular passion for a vocation, a profession, a course of action. The leader loves what he does, and loves doing it. Tolstoy said that hopes are the dreams of the waking man. We cannot survive, much less progress, without hope. The leader who communicates passion gives hope and inspiration to other people.

• **Integrity.** The next basic ingredient of leadership is integrity. I think there are three essential parts of integrity: self-knowledge, candor, and maturity.

*Self-knowledge.* "Know thyself," said the inscription over the oracle at Delphi. And it is still the most difficult task any of us faces. But until you truly know yourself, strengths and weaknesses, know what you want to do and why you want to do it, you cannot succeed in any but the most superficial sense of the word. Leaders never lie to themselves, especially about themselves, know their flaws as well as their assets, and deal with them directly. You are your own raw material. When you know what you consist of and what you want to make of it, then you can invent yourself.

*Candor.* Candor is the key to self-knowledge. Candor is based on honesty of thought and action, a steadfast devotion to principle, and a fundamental soundness and wholeness. An architect who designs a Bauhaus glass box with a Victorian cupola lacks professional integrity, as does any person who trims his principles—or even his ideas—to please. Like Lillian Hellman, the leader cannot cut his conscience to fit this year's fashions.

*Maturity.* Maturity is important to a leader because leading is not simply showing the way or issuing orders. Every leader needs to have experienced and grown through following—learning to be dedicated, observant, capable of working with and learning from others, never servile, always truthful. Having located these qualities in himself or herself, he or she can encourage them in others.

• **Trust.** Integrity is the basis of trust, which is not as much an ingredient of leadership as it is a product. It is the one quality that cannot be acquired, but must be earned. It is given by coworkers and followers, and without it, the leader can't function.

• **Curiosity and daring.** Two more basic ingredients of leadership are curiosity and daring. The leader wonders about everything, wants to learn as much as he or she can, is willing to take risks and experiment. The leader does not worry about failure, but embraces errors, knowing he or she will learn from them.

### Microwave or McLeaders

Even though I talk about basic ingredients, I'm not talking about traits that you're born with and can't change. As countless deposed kings and hapless heirs to great fortunes can attest, true leaders are not born, but made, and usually self-made. Leaders invent themselves. They are not, by the way, made in a single weekend seminar, as many of the leadership-theory spokespeople claim. I've come to think of that as the microwave theory: Pop in Mr. or Ms. Average and out pops McLeader in sixty seconds.

Billions of dollars are spent annually by and on would-be leaders. Many major corporations offer leadership development courses. Corporate America has, nevertheless, lost its lead in the world market. I would argue that more leaders have been made by accident, circumstance, sheer grit, or will than have been made by all the leadership courses put together. Leadership courses can only teach skills. They can't teach character or vision—and, indeed, they don't even try. Developing character and vision is the way leaders invent themselves.

What is true for leaders is, for better or for worse, true for each of us: We are our own raw material. Only when we know what we're made of and what we want to make of it can we begin our lives—and we must do it despite an unwitting conspiracy of people and events against us.

As television producer Norman Lear put it, "On the one hand, we're a society that seems to be proud of individuality. On the other hand, we don't really tolerate real individuality. We want to homogenize it."

### Benefits of Self-Invention for Men and Women

A couple of studies underscore the benefits, even the necessity, of self-invention. First, middle-aged men tend to change careers after having heart attacks. Faced with their own mortality, these men realize that what they've been doing, what they've invested their lives in, is not an accurate reflection of their real needs and desires.

Another study indicates that what determines the level of satisfaction in post-middle-aged men is the degree to which they acted upon their youthful dreams. It's not so much whether they were successful in achieving their dreams as the honest pursuit of them that counts. The spiritual dimension in creative effort comes from that honest pursuit.

There is, of course, evidence that women, too, are happier when they've invented themselves instead of accepting without question the roles they were brought up to play. Psychologist and author Sonya Friedman said, "The truth of the matter is that the most emotionally disturbed women are those who are married and locked into traditional full-time, lifetime homemaker roles. Single women have always been happier than married women. Always. And there isn't a study that has disproved that."

Staying single has historically been the only way most women were free to invent themselves. Nineteenth-century poet Emily Dickinson, a reclusive woman who never married and who surely invented herself, is supposed to have said to one of the rare visitors to her room, "Here is freedom!"

Fortunately, the changing times have meant changes in relationships, too. Many of the women leaders I talked with have managed to invent themselves even though married—as has Friedman herself.

### Enjoy the Journey

Norman Lear would add to this that the goal isn't worth arriving at unless you enjoy the journey. "You have to look at success incrementally," he said. "It takes too long to get to any major success. If one can look at life as doing successfully, moment by moment, one might find that most of it is successful. And take the bow inside for it. When we wait for the big bow, it's a lousy bargain. They don't come but once in too long a time."

Applauding yourself for the small successes, and taking the small bow, are good ways of learning to experience life each moment that you live it. And that's part of inventing yourself, of creating your own destiny.

To become a leader, then, you must become yourself, become the maker of your own life. It's the most rewarding task you'll ever undertake.

# 15

## LEADING FOLLOWERS, FOLLOWING LEADERS

*Charismatic or not, leaders are able to move
their people on the path of change.*

What is it that makes a person a leader? Some would say it's charisma, and you either have it or you don't. Many leaders, however, couldn't be described as particularly charismatic but nevertheless manage to inspire an enviable trust and loyalty among their followers. Through their abilities to get people on their side, they make changes in the culture of their organization and make their visions of the future real.

How do they do it? When I ask them, they talk to me about human values: empathy, trust, mutual respect—and courage.

Empathy, like charisma, may be a quality that people either have or don't have. Walt Disney producer Marty Kaplan says, "I've known leaders who have had none of it and nevertheless were leaders, but those who have had that quality have moved and inspired me more."

Former CBS executive Barbara Corday sees empathy as a special skill among women leaders:

> *I think women see power in a different way from men. I want to have the kind of power that is my company working well, my staff working well. As moms and wives and daughters, we've been caretakers, and we continue in caretaking roles even as we get successful in*

*business. I'm very proud of the fact that I not only know all the people who work for me, but I also know their husbands' and wives' names, and I know their children's names. People appreciate that, and they're loyal and care about what they're doing.*

There are plenty of male leaders who prize empathy, too. Retired Lucky Stores CEO Don Ritchey says:

*I think people are turned on when their bosses not only know they're there but know intimately what they're doing—that it's a partnership. You're trying to run this thing well together. And if something goes wrong, our goal is to fix it, not see who we can nail.*

Empathy isn't the only factor in getting people on your side. Roger Gould, founder and president of Interactive Health Systems, a computer-assisted therapy program, explains how he took charge without taking control:

*I've always been kind of a lone wolf, but when I was head of outpatient services at UCLA Medical Center, I developed a kind of consensus leadership. The fact that I was the boss didn't mean that I would or could take sole responsibility. Everyone was living with the same complexity, so we had to deal with it as a group.*

Director Sydney Pollack describes the leader's need to have people on his or her side this way:

*Up to a point, I think you can lead out of fear, intimidation, as awful as that sounds. But the problem is that you're creating obedience with a residue of resentment. If you want to make a physics analogy, you'd be moving through the medium but you'd be creating a lot of drag, a lot of backwash.*

There are two other qualities that I think are more positive reasons to follow someone. One is an honest belief in the person you're following. The other is selfish: The person following has to believe that following is the best thing to do at the time. You don't want people to follow you just because that's what they're paid for. You try to make everyone feel they have a stake in it, that they'll learn something.

### How to Be Trusted, Not Feared

Gloria Steinem, journalist and feminist leader, feels the strategy of getting people on your side makes the difference between what she calls "movement" and "corporate" leadership:

> *Movement leadership requires persuasion, not giving orders. There is no position to lead from; it doesn't exist. What makes you successful is that you can phrase things in a way that is inspirational, that makes coalition possible.*

Betty Friedan, co-founder of the National Organization for Women, endorses the idea of leading through persuasion rather than position.

> *I've never fought for organizational power," she says. "I have a great deal of influence just by my voice. I don't have to be president. I recently gave a speech at a university where only 2 percent of the faculty is women. I told the crowd, 'I must be in a place that is for some reason an anachronism.' I read the figures to them. I said, 'I'm surprised that you have not had a major class-action suit.' You could see the tension in the room. I said, 'You are really in a vulnerable position, since over 50 percent of your financing is federal funding. Just as a warning, watch it.' Then I went on with my lecture. And something happened in that room. The last ten years I haven't been the head of any organization, but I don't need to be.*

Frances Hesselbein, former executive director of the Girl Scouts and now CEO of the Peter F. Drucker Foundation, says:

> *We're not managing for the sake of being great managers; we're managing for the mission. I don't believe in a star system. I believe in helping people identify what they can do well and releasing them to do it.*

Like Friedan, Hesselbein leads with her voice. She has learned the lesson of taking charge without taking control, that she must inspire her organization's employees and volunteers, not order them.

In *Leadership Is an Art*, Max DePree, former chairman of Herman Miller, argues that this is the way to treat everyone:

> *The best people working for organizations are like volunteers. Since they could probably find good jobs in any number of groups, they choose to work somewhere for reasons less tangible than salary or position...[such as] shared commitment to ideas, to issues, to values, to goals, and to management process. Words such as love, warmth, personal chemistry, are certainly pertinent.*

### The Need for Mutual Respect

Leaders master their vocation or profession—they do whatever they do very well—but they also establish and maintain positive relationships with their subordinates inside the organization. Leaders' ability to galvanize their co-workers resides in their understanding not only of themselves, but also of their co-workers' needs and wants, along with an understanding of what can be called their mission.

"They [your co-workers] have to believe that you know what you're doing," says Don Ritchey. "You have to believe that they know what they're doing, too, and let them know that you trust them."

A major challenge that all leaders are facing now is an epidemic of corporate malfeasance. And if there is anything that undermines subordinates' trust, it is the feeling that the people at the top lack integrity, meaning they are without a solid sense of ethics.

In today's volatile business climate, leaders must steer a clear and consistent course. "I start with the presumption that most people want to be ethical," says Ritchey. "It's sort of a golden-rule philosophy. So if you set up a climate where people see that you mean it, and it works, then nobody has to make expedient choices because somebody was leaning on him, telling him on the one hand to be ethical and on the other hand to make the number even if he has to be cute about it. The fact that you are very hard-nosed about weeding out unethical behavior helps. Ethics is not Pollyanna stuff. It works better."

### Courage to Pioneer

Leading through voice, inspiring through trust and empathy,

can help create a corporate climate that gives people elbow room to do the right things and to grow. Successful leaders believe in change—in both people and organizations. They equate it with growth and progress. Change in the world at large can be an obstacle, too. "Circumstances beyond our control" is the operative phrase all too often.

Leaders may discover that the culture of their own corporations is an obstacle to the changes they want to introduce because, as currently constituted, it is devoted more to preserving itself than to meeting new challenges.

"My former boss at Pepsico and the current head of IBM were both World War II fighter pilots," says former Apple CEO John Sculley. "The fighter pilot is no longer going to be our paradigm for leaders. The new generation of leaders is going to be more intellectually aware. Beyond the ways we have to change as leaders and managers within the context of our enterprise, the world itself is changing, becoming more idea-intensive, more information-intensive; so the people who will rise to the top are going to be people who are comfortable with and excited by ideas and information."

The best leaders deal with this mercurial world by anticipating, looking not just down the road but around the corner; by seeing change as an opportunity rather than an obstacle; and by accepting it rather than resisting it.

One of the hardest lessons any novice skier has to learn is that he or she must lean away from the hill and not into it. The natural inclination is to stay as close to the slope as possible because it feels safer. But only when you lean out can you begin to control your own movements and not be controlled by the slope. The organizational novice does the same thing; leans close to the company's slope, submerging his or her own identity in that of the corporation. The leader stands tall and leans out, taking charge of his or her own course, with a clear view of where the leader is going.

### Vision & Virtue

Ultimately, a leader's ability to galvanize his or her co-workers resides both in the leader's understanding of self and understanding of co-workers' needs and wants, along with understanding of what might be called mission.

In such leaders, competence, vision, and virtue exist in near-ly perfect balance. Competence, or knowledge, without vision and virtue, breeds technocrats. Virtue, without vision and knowledge, breeds ideologues. Vision, without virtue and knowledge, breeds demagogues.

As Peter Drucker has pointed out, the chief object of leader-ship is the creation of a human community held together by the work bond for a common purpose. Organizations and their leaders inevitably deal with the nature of man, which is why values, commitments, convictions, and even passions are basic elements in any organization. Since leaders deal with people, not things, leadership without values, commitment, and con-viction can only be inhumane and harmful.

Especially today, in the current volatile climate, it is vital that leaders steer a clear and consistent course. They must acknowl-edge uncertainties and deal effectively with the present, while simultaneously anticipating and responding to the future. This means endlessly expressing, explaining, extending, expanding, and when necessary revising the organization's mission. The goals are not ends, but ideal processes by which the future can be created.

### Good Followers Make Good Leaders

It is probably inevitable that a society as star-struck as ours should focus on leaders in analyzing why organizations succeed or fail. As a longtime student and teacher of management, I, too, have tended to look to the men and women at the top for clues on how organizations achieve and maintain institutional health. But the longer I study effective leaders, the more I am persuaded of the underappreciated importance of effective fol-lowers.

What makes a good follower? The single most important characteristic may well be a willingness to tell the truth. In a world of growing complexity, leaders are increasingly dependent on their subordinates for good information, whether the leaders want to hear it or not. Followers who tell the truth, and leaders who listen to it, are an unbeatable combination.

Movie mogul Samuel Goldwyn seems to have had a gut-level awareness of the importance of what I call "effective back talk" from subordinates. After a string of box-office flops, Goldwyn called his staff together and told them: "I want you to tell me exactly what's wrong with me and MGM, even if it means losing your job." Although Goldwyn wasn't personally ready to give up the ego-massaging presence of "yes men," in his own gloriously garbled way he acknowledged the company's greater need for a staff that speaks the truth.

Like portfolios, organizations benefit from diversity. Effective leaders resist the urge to people their staffs only with others who look or sound or think just like themselves, what I call the doppelgänger, or ghostly-double, effect. They look for good people from many molds, and then they encourage them to speak out, even to disagree. Aware of the pitfalls of institutional unanimity, some leaders wisely build dissent into the decision-making process.

Organizations that encourage thoughtful dissent gain much more than a heightened air of collegiality. They make better decisions. In a recent study, Rebecca A. Henry, a psychology professor at Purdue University, found that groups were generally more effective than individuals in making forecasts of sales and other financial data. And the greater the initial disagreement among group members, the more accurate the results. "With more disagreement, people are forced to look at a wider range of possibilities," Ms. Henry said.

Like good leaders, good followers understand the importance of speaking out. More important, they do it. Almost thirty years ago, when Nikita Khrushchev came to America, he met with reporters at the Washington Press Club. The first written question he received was: "Today you talked about the hideous rule of your predecessor, Stalin. You were one of his closest aides and colleagues during those years. What were you doing all that time?" Khrushchev's face grew red. "Who asked that?" he roared. No one answered. "Who asked that?" he insisted. Again, silence. "That's what I was doing," Khrushchev said.

Even in democracies where the only gulag is the threat of a pink slip, it is hard to disagree with the person in charge. Several years ago TV's John Chancellor asked former presidential aides how they behaved on those occasions when the most powerful person in the world came up with a damned fool idea. Several of the aides admitted doing nothing. Ted Sorenson revealed that John F. Kennedy could usually be brought to his senses by being told, "That sounds like the kind of idea Nixon would have."

Quietism, as a more pious age called the sin of silence, often costs organizations—and their leaders—dearly. Former President Ronald Reagan suffered far more at the hands of so-called friends who refused to tell him unattractive truths than from his ostensible enemies.

Nancy Reagan, in her memoir, *My Turn*, recalls chiding then-Vice President George Bush when he approached her, not the President, with grave reservations about White House chief of staff Donald Regan. "I wish you'd tell my husband," the First Lady said. "I can't be the only one who's saying this to him." According to Mrs. Reagan, Bush responded, "Nancy, that's not my role."

"That's exactly your role," she snapped.

Nancy Reagan was right. It is the good follower's obligation to share his or her best counsel with the person in charge. And silence—not dissent—is the one answer that leaders should refuse to accept. History contains dozens of cautionary tales on the subject, none more vivid than the account of the murder of Thomas of Becket. "Will no one rid me of this meddlesome priest?" Henry II muttered, after a contest of wills with his former friend.

The four barons who then murdered Becket in his cathedral were the antithesis of the good followers they thought themselves to be. At the risk of being irreverent, the right answer to Henry's question—the one that would have served his administration best—was "No," or at least "Let's talk about it."

Like modern-day subordinates who testify under oath that they were only doing what they thought their leader wanted them to do, the barons were guilty of remarkable chutzpa. Henry failed by not making his position clear and by creating an atmosphere in which his followers would rather kill than disagree with him. The barons failed by not making the proper case against the king's decision.

Effective leaders reward dissent, as well as encourage it. They understand that whatever momentary discomfort they experience as a result of being told from time to time that they are wrong is more than offset by the fact that reflective back talk increases a leader's ability to make good decisions.

Executive compensation should go far toward salving the pricked ego of the leader whose followers speak their minds. But what's in it for the follower? The good follower may indeed have to put his or her job on the line in the course of speaking up. But consider the price he or she pays for silence. What job is worth the enormous psychiatric cost of following a leader who values loyalty in the narrowest sense?

Perhaps the ultimate irony is that the follower who is willing to speak out shows precisely the kind of initiative that leadership is made of.

# 16

## PERILS OF ACCORD,
## ADVANTAGES OF ACCESS

*We need some fresh faces and voices to renew organizations
and regain advantage, but we can't seem to find any.*

Do corporations in this volatile era function more effectively on accord or discord?

I happen to think that too much accord is always perilous and usually false. Two of this country's most effective executives, Jim Burke at Johnson & Johnson and Andrew Grove at Intel, insist on what they describe as "creative confrontation" with their associates. They not only encourage dissent in their executive suite, they demand it, and they surround themselves with people smart enough to know the truth and independent enough to speak it—especially when it's at apparent odds with their own perceptions.

If corporate officers are to function in the real world, then they have to live and work in the real world, never insulating or isolating themselves or surrounding themselves with people too much like themselves.

Just as they expect dissent, disagreement, and truth from their associates, effective executives go in search of the truth themselves, spending considerable time in the field, looking at their own operations, talking with their workers and their customers. The great German composer and conductor Gustav Mahler insisted that each principal musician in the orchestra sit in the audience at least once a week to get some sense of the whole.

117

Effective executives, no matter how high they rise, remain inquisitive, curious about everything. They read, go around, look, explore, wonder, make connections, always know that their company is not the whole but only part of it. They are by nature restless, never satisfied, ever aware that there is no such thing as perfection, convinced that any product can be improved and any procedure upgraded. Furthermore, effective executives know that the world is not static but dynamic, in a constant state of flux. They are committed to change.

Effective executives' priorities are very clear, and, appropriately enough, the bottom line is the last thing on their minds, while the first order of business is customer satisfaction. Customer satisfaction derives from good products and services, which in turn derive from talented, committed workers. Satisfied customers, talented and committed workers, and first-rate products and services inevitably add up and make the company profitable, but effective executives continue to look and listen in an effort to see, hear, and understand the world as it is, and as it is becoming. Corporations remain alive and alert and unblinded by their own success, then, to the degree that the people in charge remain alive and alert to the world.

### Canceling the Doppelgänger Effect

One of the most striking things about white-collar crimes is how much all the conspirators resemble one another in manner, posture, and speech, as if they were all doppelgängers, ghostly doubles. This idea was suggested to me by one of my mentors, Herbert A. Shepard.

This doppelgängers phenomenon is by no means an accident. If spy cameras zoomed in on the headquarters of any large bureaucracy—in either the public or the private sector—they would see the effect repeated endlessly, because by and large people tend to select people to work with them who are cut from the same goods. What's worse, if the cameras zoomed in on any watering hole in any more or less affluent section of any city or suburb in America, they would find dozens of look-alikes.

Many CEOs tend to choose assistants who resemble them not only in ideas and attitudes but in height, stature, and dress; in fact, one corporation's campus recruiters are required to note whether prospective employees "look like us."

The desire for a congenial and closely knit management group is quite human and even understandable. The sheer size of organizations makes it impossible for the top people to verify their own information, analyze their own problems, and decide whom they should spend their time with. They have to rely on their assistants to double for them in certain instances, and so, to a degree, those assistants should be of kindred minds and compatible natures. Assistants are the inevitable products of big business and are indispensable, but since they control access to their boss, choosing both the material and people the boss will see, they control the boss to an extent. There are two problems inherent in the system: 1) things the boss needs to know and people the boss needs to see may be kept from him or her by overzealous assistants—either out of eagerness to protect the boss or out of simple ignorance; and 2) they may, in the same spirit, exercise more authority than they have.

The one thing a president needs above all is the truth, all of it, all the time, and it is the one thing a president is least likely to get from his assistants, if they are cut from the same cloth. Pierre du Pont once wrote:

> *One cannot expect to know what will happen, one can only consider himself fortunate if he can learn what has happened.*

I was president for six years of the University of Cincinnati, and I was blessed with a staff of dedicated, honest, and intelligent men and women, with whom I had to endlessly struggle for the whole truth and nothing but the truth. When I finally pried whatever it was I needed to know out of them, they would say things like, "Well, I didn't want to bother you," or "I didn't want to call you wrong in front of other people," or "I didn't want to burden you," or "I thought you were making a mistake, but I didn't want to argue with you." To paraphrase the old saying, with assistants like these, who needs enemies? I believed, during my Cincinnati tenure, that the buck indeed stopped in my office, but I was lucky to be able to find the buck, much less learn where it had stopped outside my office, and why.

Obviously, then, the top people have to surround themselves with people who can, first, recognize the truth when they see it and, second, convey it to them, whether they want to hear it or not.

### Allowing Access

Corporate CEOs are often prevented from meeting with people because their assistants make snap judgments. Imagine what might have happened if Albert Einstein, in his usual sweatshirt and sneakers, had turned up at the White House to see President Roosevelt and encountered a 1930s version of Robert Haldeman, Nixon's majordomo. Einstein not only would not have been allowed in, he would probably have been jailed as a "suspicious character."

To ensure that they have access to the people and things they need to know, presidents of organizations should institute some simple rules:

• Rotate your key assistants every two years to ensure less arrogance, more humility, and continuing openness.

• Ensure all assistants have sufficient contact with their general constituency so that they understand both the obligations and the limits of power.

• Run away from the doppelgänger effect. However comforting loyalty and congeniality are, they are not sufficient. Assistants should be as diverse in viewpoint and background as possible.

• Read at least one daily newspaper and don't rely exclusively on staff summaries for your information. If you hear only what you want to hear and find only what you want to find you will soon find yourself in trouble.

• Don't rely exclusively on your intimates for information. Anyone who is in charge of an organization must be accessible to its members and its constituents. When an old woman accosted the Roman emperor Hadrian, he brushed her aside, saying that he was too busy. She replied, "Then you're too busy to be emperor," whereupon he stopped and heard her out. The president who only talks and never listens will soon have nothing to say to anyone. E.M. Forster wrote, "Only connect." And that, after all, is any CEO's primary responsibility.

It is the excessive zeal, the concealments, the arrogances and half-truths of thousands of faceless doppelgängers in hundreds of organizations—from the White House to the corner hardware store—that set off troubles. The truth may hurt, but it doesn't kill anyone.

Then there are all those other doppelgängers—the yuppies who look alike, dress alike, think alike, and think mostly about acquiring more money and more things. Fundamentally in it for themselves, incapable of continuing loyalty to people, causes, or organizations, they have no interest in honesty or truth, either. Unable to lead, unwilling to follow, they merely copy, but their models are as bogus as they are, and as crass. These are the hollow people, the empty suits who have mastered the art of taking without ever giving, which may be why so many of them seem to wind up in jail. The presence of these moral zombies in our midst is the most obvious manifestation of our decline into anarchy. So let us be angry at the state of the union, and let us begin to connect.

### Employing Cormorants

When asked what wisdom the ancient Oriental philosophers could pass along to modern man, Dr. Ralph Siu offered a list of "advices."

One went as follows: "Observe the cormorant in the fishing fleet. You know how cormorants are used for fishing. The technique involves a man in a rowboat with about a half-dozen cormorants, each with a ring about its neck. When the bird spots a fish, it dives into the water and catches the fish in its beak. The ring prevents the larger fish from being swallowed, so the fisherman takes the fish from the cormorant, which then dives for another fish."

Why is it, Dr. Siu asked, of all the animals the cormorant has been chosen to slave away for the fisherman? If the bird were not greedy for the fish, efficient in catching it and readily trainable, would society have created an industry to exploit it? Or would the ingenious ring have been devised? Of course not. Thus, Dr. Siu concludes, greed, talent and capacity for learning become the bases for exploitation. Institutions and organizations are designed to make society, not the individual, prosper. Therefore, society encourages greed, talent and the capacity for learning in us, then puts rings around our necks and makes cormorants of us.

How can we simultaneously exercise our ambition, talent and capacity for learning, and contribute to society and its organizations and institutions without becoming cormorants, doing the work but never enjoying the intrinsic benefits of the work?

Our parents, our schools and our organizations all inadvertently conspire against us when they focus on the development of a career, with the rest of life merely an unanticipated consequence of the career, or even when they stress the how-tos of a career rather than the whys.

Don Juan was explicit about this in teaching Carlos Casteneda about careers. To have a path of knowledge, a path with a heart, made for a joyful journey, he said, and was the only conceivable way to live. We must think carefully about our paths before we set out on them, for by the time a person discovers that his path "has no heart," the path is ready to kill him.

At that point, few of us have the courage to abandon the path, lethal as it may be, because we have invested so much in it, have become so successful at it, and to choose a new path seems dangerous, even irresponsible, and so we continue dutifully, if joylessly, along. Being the natural or adopted descendants of Puritans, we remain suspicious of joy anyway, and comfortable, to an extent, in our rings.

But it seems appropriate for all of us to consider not only slipping out of the rings we've worn willingly ourselves, but also not encumbering our new young employees with rings.

### Lessons from Great Leaders

As I delved into the workings of leadership—super leaders, people of enormous and, in some cases, exquisite achievements in the arts, athletics and public life, as well as industry—I discovered several things.

First, true leaders lead fully integrated lives, in which their careers and their personal lives fit seamlessly and harmoniously together. Professional and private activities complement and enhance each other.

Second, true leaders have never been cormorants, even for a moment. Their ambition, talent and capacity to learn have served them, rather than enslaving them.

Third, by using their ambition, talent and capacity, these leaders have identified their true calling, as it were, and fulfilled their own genius, their visions of excellence through the application of passion, energy and focus. Moreover, as the leader has learned to fulfill his or her own vision, he or she has also assisted employees to fulfill their own visions. This is a less altruistic process than you might think.

The cormorant is merely efficient, but the freed bird is inspired to achieve everything he is capable of doing, and there isn't a company in America that wouldn't benefit from a little less efficiency and a lot more inspiration.

It isn't always easy to set the visions of one's employees loose. After all, they have been through the mill, too, and have, in many cases, chosen their own rings. For example, a young man may have learned early that he had a gift for numbers and therefore chosen the path of numbers, without even bothering to test his other talents. You may see in your young numbers man a flair for design, but the very idea of moving into unknown territory may seem frightening to him, and so he may resist.

You then find yourself facing a difficult choice. Either you can persist, pushing him to fulfill his true talents, or you can withdraw and settle for his more commonplace skills. Real leaders, of course, persist, because they are unwilling to settle for anything less than the best—in themselves, their organizations, and their employees.

In this way, a leader's passion, energy and focus begets a passion, energy and focus in the leader's workers. Watch a great conductor or football coach in action and you will see what I mean. The members of the orchestra or the team are not dutiful, but inspired.

### Imagination and Vision

The '80s were not a good decade for American business, and at least part of the problem resided in its elevation of obedience over imagination. Ironically, the very businesses which suffered the most, such as the auto industry, were founded by men who were far more imaginative than they were obedient. By the same token, those businesses which flourished, such as the computer industry, cared little for obedience, but put a premium on imagination. America itself emerged out of simultaneous disobedience and vision.

But, in the current climate, vision is a fragile thing, and needs to be nourished and developed in you as well as your employees and co-workers.

It isn't easy, of course, or without risks, which is why too many executives prefer to deal with simple day-to-day problems and settle for small wins, rather than trying to deal with the overarching problems. But, as I see it, one of the greatest threats to American business, perhaps the ultimate threat, is its narrowing of horizons, its tendency to restrict its vision and devote its principal energies to just hanging in there, denying the sense of wide-ranging possibilities, of entire worlds to conquer what used to animate American business and made it one of the wonders of the world.

This narrowing of horizons has, of course, been noticed by our young people, and is reflected now in their own attitudes. More and more young people are merely ambitious, even greedy, and perfectly willing to play the cormorant. An ophthalmologist, a leader in his field, told me not long ago that the young people entering his profession scared him to death. "They care nothing for the work, only for the money. One told me that he chose the field because it meant short office hours, no emergencies, and a lot of money for a little work." I asked him how these young people had gotten so greedy. He said, "They grew up in a greedy world. It's all they know."

We have all participated in the making of this ever-narrowing world, and it is time now that we work to unmake it, by freeing ourselves and our fellow workers, if for no other reason than that it isn't working.

As technology advances on every front, as our tools become more accomplished and more sophisticated, we are more capable than ever of realizing our visions, even our more extravagant visions. Yet the more we are able to do, the less we seem to do. We are in danger of becoming, in Thoreau's words, "the tools of our tools," mere operators rather than explorers, mechanics rather than inventors.

The world doesn't need any more operators or mechanics, but it desperately needs explorers and inventors—people willing to take on the world and its problems by living up to their own visions of excellence and using their talents to the full. Again, this isn't as altruistic as it seems.

Anyone who isn't fulfilling himself because he's fearful of failing or making a fool of himself isn't happy, any more than the cormorant is happy, however successful he may be.

As literary critic John Mason Brown once said, "The only true happiness comes from squandering yourselves for a purpose." America in general, and American business in particular, needs more squanderers, and fewer cormorants.

# 17

# LEADING FOR RESULTS

*Today's climate is so filled with contradictions, dilemmas, and ambiguities that it's making life tough for every executive.*

At age 68 I took my first sabbatical in 45 years. Of course, my colleagues claimed I'd always been on sabbatical. I spent my time writing a one-act play; taking yoga; learning the computer; making my marriage work; writing a book on creative collaboration; and taking singing lessons. My singing coach assigned "It Had to Be You" as my first song. I told him anyone who messed up that song should be subject to the death penalty. He told me to get ready. But I felt I was finally cresting. I thought about me and Clint Eastwood, Bertrand Russell, and Mel Torme—all in our late sixties—we just keep trying for more.

I'm just glad I still have a job. Look around. CEOs are being dumped in unprecedented numbers. The forces of size, speed, and change intersect to create ineptitude, inertia, and arrogance. Democratization, capitalism, the growth of technology, and the problems of oversupply on their own are major change forces. Combined, they have created an environment of seismic change. Finding people who can lead in such an environment is challenging. You need people who can walk their companies into the future, not back them into the future.

### Learning Environments
The key to gaining a competitive advantage today will be

the ability of leaders to create an adaptive, learning environment that encourages the development of intellectual capital. Leaders must learn how to create environments that release the creative powers of individuals. Many of the CEOs who were pushed out didn't have that ability. Leadership is learned on the job. Leaders learn to be leaders. They learn by facing and overcoming challenges—learning from mistakes and going forward. They learn the most from their bosses—both good and bad ones.

Why don't organizations do a better job of creating leaders? One reason is that leaders challenge the system; they question the gospel. In times of change, most organizations don't reward such behavior; they reward managers who follow. Author George Bernard Shaw said: "All great progress is made by unreasonable men who make the world adapt to them; and reasonable men adapt to the world."

Too few executives are asking themselves: "How do we build leaders for the future?" We know that the more horizontal assignments a person gets, the more leadership talent the person develops. So involve potential leaders in every aspect of the business throughout their careers.

Coaching will become the model for leaders in the future. Coaches teach, mentor, and empower. You have to be honest with coaches, and they with you, if you are to grow. They help you focus on what's important now. All organizations need leaders to remind them every day what's important now—at the same time they are defining a vision of the future.

In leaders, character matters. Leadership is composed of ambition, competence, and integrity. Imagine someone with just unbridled ambition—and you get a demagogue. Imagine someone with just competence—and you get a leader who destroys the soul of the organization. In picking a leader, always insist on integrity. Sadly, in times of turbulence, people often pick a leader who has ambition and competence, but little integrity or moral fabric. Ultimately, those leaders fail, and their followers pay an enormous price.

With all the restructuring going on, leaders find it hard to maintain or regain trust. Sadly, many leaders put themselves in the position where they have to regain trust. A reduction in jobs is never popular. However, a leader doesn't have to pay for change with trust if his communication about change is honest and open, candid and caring. You can no longer promise job security, but you can promise and deliver employability by providing people with the skills and training they need to work, either at your organization or another one. If you do that, and explain it well, you won't lose the trust of your employees.

### Releasing the Brainpower

Executives, before they restructure, must learn to use the brainpower of their people. How do you empower people when you are going through restructuring, downsizing, and reengineering? How do you maintain relationships with those who stay and those who leave? This is where we need re-education to handle the dislocation and transition.

The primary task of leadership is to create a structure that releases the brainpower of people and transmits ideas fast. I don't know what that form looks like, but several evolving structures—including temporary systems, cluster organizations, loosely coupled organizations, networks, and teams—provide some clues. But it clearly isn't bureaucracy—the mind-set of control, order, and predict. I suppose that it doesn't matter what the form is; whatever people want to work, will work. But I suspect that it's going to be a form that aligns, creates, and empowers.

One way leaders release the brainpower and creativity of people is to create effective forms of organization. MasterCard International is evolving into a federation where decisions are made by the units that can best make them. The only reason for decisions to get made at the top is when the matter to be decided is something that relates to everybody, or you need some sort of synergy among the units. We need to think of new forms, and federation is one of the best in terms of its potential to accommodate the nature of global business.

No business will succeed without placing high emphasis on people. I see the role of human resources changing as more people heading up human resources are coming from the operations side of business. This is a good sign because the rap against human resources has always been that HR people did not understand how the business operated. As that changes, the role of HR will grow in importance. In a climate of restructuring, reengineering, and downsizing, the major emphasis must be on wisely managing an organization's investment in people. And that role falls squarely in human resources.

Some 25 years ago, I thought rigid, pyramidal organizations were doomed, largely for theoretical reasons. Now I see they are doomed because they simply do not work or, more precisely, because they do not work fast enough. Today's most viable institutions are dancers, not marchers.

All effective leaders reinvent themselves as they go along. True leaders are constant learners. They hunger for knowledge. They learn from every position. And they grow both in knowledge and in character. They learn from mistakes and become effective. In a sense, most successful people reinvent themselves through continuous learning.

Once a Polish visionary claimed to see a synagogue burning to the ground in a village some 45 miles away. When a man from that village appeared the next day to say that the synagogue was untouched by fire, that hardly bothered the local citizens. "So what if he was wrong," they said of their visionary. "Look how far he could see."

I don't think the fierce galloping toward globalization or the development of advanced technology would have been so difficult to foresee. Some leaders were able to foresee these developments, or hint of them. Successful leaders recognize that we're moving to a stage of idea-intensive production and away from material-intensive production. They realize that success comes through intellectual capital that creates wealth; and that people with ideas are going to make a difference. What leaders offer is intellectual capital, ideas, know-how. They create a learning environment—an adaptive, agile, athletic, social architecture capable of generating intellectual capital.

Great leaders are concerned with people, dollars, and ideas. If they pick the right people and allocate the right number of dollars to particular divisions, and if they break down the bureaucratic roles so the best practices get transferred immediately from one division to the next—then we're going to see successful corporations. Successful corporations will not be content to rest on their past success. They will change, reorganize, and revitalize without being forced to. There is a correlation between the size of a company and its capacity to change. It's the difference between turning around the Queen Mary and a speedboat. Large companies have thick walls between divisions that make passing information and ideas back and forth difficult.

A new leader has emerged who is a facilitator, not an autocrat; an appreciator of ideas, not a fount of them. These leaders realize that they're basically coaches. I once asked Jack Welch, "How can you make decisions about everything from light bulbs to computers to turbine engines to medical instrumentation?" He replied, "I don't. My job isn't to go to Louisville to pick the color of the refrigerator, or decide on the size of the door handle or which way it turns. My job is to ask questions. Can the Italians make it more cheaply, for instance? Or should we outsource it? All I do is ask questions, bringing up ideas, and in the process transferring them out."

Good leaders have moved away from being macho to being maestros, conductors bringing out the best in each member of the orchestra. If a leader wants to keep the best and the brightest, if he or she wants a company that has its foundation in ideas, innovation, and learning, the leader's got to be the coach who gets people to play at their best, who brings out the best of their ideas. That's what it's all about—ideas. Many competitors have no resources or unique technology. What they have is the ability to utilize their people, using their brains. That's what it takes today.

# 18

## LEARNING TO LEAD

*My basic premise is that learning to be an effective leader is
no different from learning to be an effective person.*

People often ask me, "How do you grow a leader?" I must
confess: I don't understand all that goes into developing leaders. If I had a recipe, I'd win the Nobel prize. While there is
general agreement about the qualities of leadership, the question of how we grow leaders is moot. Here's the deal: Learning
is virtually the same process as becoming an integrated,
healthy person. Or as Shakespeare put it, "Learning is but an
adjunct of our selves." What that means is that when we talk
about "growing leaders," we're inevitably involved in personal
transformation.

### Facilitating Learning

While I don't think you can "teach" leadership, I am certain that leadership can be learned and that terrific coaches
can create some experiential setups to facilitate learning.
Coaching is the rub. Giving advice or feedback that may
improve the performance of the recipient while maintaining
her or his self-esteem is the hard part. How can a coach learn
to be supportive and not controlling? I suppose that question
must come up continually for anyone in the "helping professions." In one study, over 4,000 executives were asked how
candid and open they are in giving feedback to their "direct
reports." Almost none claimed to be as open and honest as

they could be.

Despite the fact that all leaders and managers have a stock-pile of improvement advice, they don't offer it either because they feel it won't be followed or because they fear that the recipients will perceive it as a criticism and a provocation of hostility. So, all too often, management turns into a manipula-tive art where deception, spin, maneuvering, guided ambiguity, and other small deceits and slights of the tongue replace straightforward communication.

Incidentally, subordinates have an equally difficult time giv-ing their bosses helpful advice. About 70 percent of the hun-dreds of executives I've surveyed over the past fifteen years do not offer feedback or advice that is at an angle to the norms and preferences of the boss, even when they know that following a certain course will lead to disaster.

So the first rule in any coaching is that the coach has to engage in "deep listening," meaning that the coach must relate to the context in which the "other" is reasoning—they must "tune in" to where the other is "coming from."

The basis of leadership is the capacity of the leader to change the mind-set, the framework of another person. Of course, that's not easy. Most of us think that we tune into the other person, when usually we listen most intently to ourselves.

### Experiential Learning

People learn about leadership experientially. There are two major sources of learning: the individual and the organization-al setting. Individuals must have the ambition to become lead-ers. Without that motivation, as is true in almost every walk of life, nothing will work.

I should add that one must be aware of the Richard III syn-drome: Be wary of people who can't live without power—the drive for power without purpose.

Assuming individuals have a healthy aspiration for leader-ship, they must develop the capacity to learn from positive and negative experience. I often ask my clients to keep a careful diary of their leadership or "influence attempts." We can then discuss their notes. More valuable is direct feedback. Frequently, I "shadow" the person, observe carefully, and try to supply helpful information. What most of us need, leaders or not, is "reflective backtalk" from people we respect.

I suspect that we learn the most facing adversity. People who face adversity and grow from it have all the makings of becoming effective leaders. One woman CEO I interviewed said, "It wasn't until I hit bottom twice that the iron entered my soul and turned into the steel and resilience I needed."

There's also something that can be called a "propitious moment," when something is said that has special resonance for you. So a novel, play, poem, or painting may "change your life." But I'm willing to wager that it was a propitious moment, based on some synchronicity between imagination and experience.

What can an organization do to facilitate and accelerate the competencies of its leaders? Here are four simple things:

**1. Provide terrific role models.** Modeling is one of the best ways to "teach" leadership. That goes for good and bad role models. Often, we learn the most from negative role models.

**2. Identify and reward effective coaches.** I know of no organization that does it exceptionally well, even in this day when coaching is so highly touted.

**3. Rotate individuals who have the potential for leadership to a variety of roles and jobs.** I'm talking about horizontal mobility, not just moving up the ladder. We learn a lot about ourselves and others by changing positions. Incidentally, overseas experience turns out to be one of the best precursors of effective leadership, perhaps because such experience expands perspective and opens one to options.

**4. Provide potential leaders with experiences that will benefit them.** Appoint them to chair task forces that consist of a wide range of people, both in terms of status and position. Leading such a group effectively relies on persuasion, not coercion; on supporting, not controlling.

# 19

## HOW LEADERS LEARN

*Conventional learning accepts conventional wisdom; leaders engage in innovative learning to solve problems and break barriers.*

One of the problems with standard leadership courses is that they focus exclusively on skills and produce managers rather than leaders, if they produce anything at all.

Managerial skills can, of course, be taught. And they are useful skills for leaders to have. The ingredients of leadership cannot be taught, however. They must be learned. As CalFed CEO Robert Dockson put it: "The things that matter most can't be taught in a formal classroom setting." Walter Wriston at Citicorp and A.P. Giannini at the Bank of America weren't technicians. They were men of vision. They knew what they wanted to do and where they wanted to take their companies.

Since by definition each leader is unique, what leaders learn and how they use it to shape the future are unique. But to understand how leaders learn, it is important to look at some ideas about learning itself.

In 1972, the Club of Rome began a study of learning, opening with a delineation of outer limits, which, in its words, "narrow our possibilities of material growth on a finite planet," and closing with a defense of "the inner free margins . . . which exist in ourselves and are pregnant with the potency of unparalleled developments."

The Club's report was published in 1979 as *No Limits to Learning: Bridging the Human Gap,* by James W. Botkin, Mahdi

Elmandjra, and Mircea Malitza. Aurelio Peccei states in his foreword, "All we need at this point in human evolution is to learn what it takes to learn what we should learn—and learn it."

The authors go on to define "the human gap" as "the distance between growing complexity and our capacity to cope with it . . . We call it a human gap because it is a dichotomy between a growing complexity of our own making and a lagging development of our own capacities."

### Conventional Learning

The authors describe the two principal modes of conventional learning:

*Maintenance learning,* the most prevalent, is "the acquisition of fixed outlooks, methods and rules for dealing with known and recurring situations. . . . It is the type of learning designed to maintain an existing system or established way of life."

*Shock learning,* almost as prevalent now, occurs when events overwhelm people. As the authors put it, "Even up to the present moment, humanity continues to wait for events and crises that catalyze or impose this primitive learning by shock. Shock learning can be seen as a product of elitism, technocracy and authoritarianism. Learning by shock often follows a period of overconfidence in solutions created solely with expert knowledge or technical competence and perpetuated beyond the conditions for which they were appropriate."

In other words, both maintenance learning and shock learning are less learning than they are accepting conventional wisdom. Society or one's family or school says this is the way things are and these are the things you need to know, and you accept what you're told as gospel. You forget that there is a self that must be listened to.

America's automotive industry prospered on maintenance learning, until it suddenly found itself up against the wall, outdone and outsold by the Japanese automotive wizards, and learned by shock that it was in crisis. Detroit was bankrupt creatively and facing financial ruin, but instead of trying to think its way out of the dilemma, it ran on shock for years, closing down plants, throwing thousands of employees out of work, buying any solution that looked good. Only in the last year or two has Detroit begun to truly recover from its self-inflicted wounds, and the key to the recovery has been what the Club of Rome calls "innovative learning."

The authors write, "The conventional pattern of maintenance/shock learning is inadequate to cope with global complexity and is likely, if unchecked, to lead to . . . loss of control over events and crises."

What applies on a global basis applies on the personal level, too. Anyone who relies on maintenance and shock learning is bound to be more reactor than actor in his or her own life. For example, most families simply maintain. When someone in the family dies suddenly, the shock is so profound that the family frequently falls apart, at least temporarily. We all know husbands and wives who were so devastated by the death of a child that they wound up divorced.

In the same way, anyone in business who simply accepts conventional wisdom may reach the top of a bureaucratic organization, but they will never use their particular talents to their fullest, and if they ever confront their lives, they will suffer the shock of failed aspirations—at the very least.

### Innovative Learning

For leaders, innovative learning must replace maintenance and shock learning. The principal components of innovative learning are:

• anticipation: being active and imaginative rather than passive and habitual.

• learning by listening to others.

• participation: shaping events, rather than being shaped by them.

In making what the authors of the Club of Rome report call "the shift from unconscious adaptation to conscious participation," we make or recognize new connections, generating useful syntheses, and our understanding deepens.

Movie director Sydney Pollack discussed the forces that work against innovative learning:

> *Everybody has the ability to free associate, but society tends to frown on active fantasies. Beyond a certain age, we stop playing games, "let's pretend," "what if," and all that. It goes on in your head anyway, but at some point you start to feel guilty. You listen to a sym-*

*phony and imagine that you're the conductor, and there you are, conducting like crazy, but then you get to be a grown man, and you say, "Gee, I'd hate for anybody to know that I'm pretending I'm conducting the symphony." But that fantasy life is the real key to problem-solving at every level. It's certainly the primary tool for problem-solving in art, whether it's painting or dancing or choreography or directing films or writing scripts or writing novels or whatever.*

Creative problem-solving is one form of innovative learning.

Innovative learning is a way to perceive complexity. American foreign policy was skewed for a generation because our policymakers operated on the false assumption that communism was monolithic. It was a textbook example of maintenance learning. In fact, there are as many varieties of communism as there are of democracy. Maintenance learning sees communism as purely political, rather than social, economic, and political. Innovative learning sees through the political similarities to the social and economic differences that divide communist societies.

Maintenance learning, which most organizations and educational institutions practice, seeks to preserve the status quo and make good soldiers of us all. It's a monologue based in authority, hierarchical, exclusive, and solitary. Being limited and finite, it is a static body of knowledge. It requires us to adjust to things as they are.

Shock learning keeps us in line and obedient, by confirming our inability to control events or prepare for the future as individuals, and by affirming the need for authority and hierarchical organizations to protect us.

Innovative learning is the primary means of exercising one's autonomy, a means of understanding and working within the prevailing context in a positive way. It is a dialogue that begins with curiosity and is fueled by knowledge, leading to understanding. It is inclusive, unlimited, and unending, knowing and dynamic. It allows us to change the way things are.

Through the exercise of innovative learning, we no longer follow along, but rather lead our own lives. We do not accept things as they are, but rather anticipate things as they can be. We start to make new things happen. We have begun the process of becoming a leader.

### Learning from Adversity

Robert Abboud was once fired from the top slot in a Chicago bank. He went to work for Armand Hammer and was fired again. Then he moved to Texas and became CEO of the First National Bankcorp.

When asked how he could account for his success after all that failure, he cited an exchange on "The Andy Griffith Show" that summed it up: Barney, Andy's deputy, asked Andy how one acquired good judgment. Andy said he guessed it came from experience. Barney asked how you got experience. Andy said, "You get kicked around a little bit." Abboud shrugged and said, "I got kicked around a little bit."

Abboud learned from his experience, rather than being defeated by it, because he didn't simply accept it. He reflected on it, understood it, and used it. Leaders learn by doing—they learn where there are challenges, where the task is unprogrammed, where the job is being done for the first time. How do you rescue a bank? You learn by doing it. You learn through all the things that happen on the job.

Some people call this learning from adversity. But I don't think of it that way. I think of it as learning from surprise.

Sydney Pollack told me how he learned from experience. "The first time I ever directed anything," he said, "I acted like a director. That's the only thing I knew how to do, because I didn't know anything about directing. I had images of directors from working with them, and I even tried to dress like a director—clothes that were kind of outdoorsy. I didn't put on puttees, or anything like that. But if there had been a megaphone around, I would have grabbed it."

### Grow in Office

One of a leader's principal gifts is his or her ability to use experience to grow in office. Teddy Roosevelt was described as "a clown" before he became president. His cousin, Franklin D. Roosevelt, was dismissed by Walter Lippman as "a pleasant country squire who wants to be president." The Roosevelts are now regarded as two of this country's best presidents. For leaders, the test and the proof are always in the doing.

Leaders learn by leading, and they learn best by leading in the face of obstacles. As weather shapes mountains, so problems make leaders. Difficult bosses, lack of vision and virtue in the executive suite, circumstances beyond their control, and their own mistakes have been the leaders' basic curriculum.

Korn/Ferry co-founder Richard Ferry belongs to what might be called the throw-them-into-the-water-and-they'll-learn-to-swim school: "You can't really create leaders. How do you teach people to make decisions, for example? All you can do is develop the talents people have. I'm a great believer in trial by fire, on-the-job experience. Put them out there in the plants, put them in the markets, send them to Japan and Europe. Train them on the job."

According to a study by behavioral scientists Michael Lombardo and Morgan McCall at the Center for Creative Leadership, adversity is as random—and as prevalent—as good luck. After interviewing nearly 100 top executives, they found that serendipity was the rule, not the exception, and that the executives' ascensions were anything but orderly. Key events included radical job changes and serious problems, as well as lucky breaks. Problems cited included failure, demotions, missed promotions, assignments overseas, starting new businesses from scratch, corporate mergers, takeovers and shakeups, and office politics.

Lombardo and McCall concluded that adversity instructs, that successful executives ask endless questions, that they surpass their less successful compatriots primarily because they learn more from all their experiences, and that they learn early in their careers to be comfortable with ambiguity.

Television producer Norman Lear, too, sees obstacles as an integral part of leadership:

> *To be an effective leader, you not only have to get the group of followers on the right path, but you must be able to convince them that whatever obstacle stands in the way ahead, whether it's a tree or a building that blocks the view, you're going to get around it. You're not going to be put off by the apparent barriers to your goal. All journeys are filled with potholes and mines, but the only way we can move beyond them is to approach them, and recognize them for what they are.*

*You have to see that it's only a tree, or whatever, and it's not insurmountable. Everywhere you trip is where the treasure lies.*

That's learning from surprise, as well as adversity. Virtually every leader I've talked with would agree.

A number of them learned valuable lessons from difficult bosses—some even from bad bosses. The difference between the two is that bad bosses teach you what not to do. The difficult boss offers more complex lessons. A difficult boss can be challenging, picky, intimidating, arrogant, abrupt, and mercurial. But at the same time he can inspire, provide vision, and occasionally even care about you.

A classic example of a difficult boss is Robert Maxwell, a true visionary—and a successful one—who admitted to all of those flaws listed above during a "60 Minutes" interview. He once fired his son for forgetting to pick him up at the airport, and then rehired him six months later.

The ideal boss for a growing leader is probably a good boss with major flaws, so that one can learn all the complex lessons of what to do and what not to do simultaneously.

### Bouncing Back

Ernest Hemingway said that the world breaks all of us, and we grow stronger in the broken places. That's certainly true of leaders. Their capability to rebound permits them to achieve, to realize their vision.

CalFed CEO Robert Dockson told me of the time he was fired by the Bank of America: "It was one of the best things that ever happened to me, because if you can bounce back, you can learn a great deal."

This brings me to what I think of as the Wallenda Factor, a concept I described in detail in *Leaders* and so will recap only briefly here. Shortly after the great aerialist Karl Wallenda fell to his death in 1978 while doing his most dangerous walk, his wife, also an aerialist, said, "All Karl thought about for months before was falling. It was the first time he'd ever thought about that, and it seemed to me that he put all his energies into not falling rather than walking the tightrope." If we think more about failing at what we're doing than about doing it, we will not succeed.

Few other American leaders—none that I talked with—have experienced anything like the Tylenol crisis that Jim Burke had to deal with several years ago. It was a calamity that could have destroyed Johnson & Johnson, but both the company and Burke emerged stronger and wiser than before. Burke talked to me at length about the crisis, and it was clear that at no moment did he think about not succeeding.

Our leaders transform experience into wisdom and, in turn, transform the cultures of their organizations. In this way, society as a whole is transformed. It is neither a tidy nor necessarily logical process, but it's the only one we have.

There is magic in experience, as well as wisdom. And more magic in stress, challenge, and adversity, and more wisdom. And the letters JOB after one's name mean infinitely more to the wise than all the BAs, MBAs, and Ph.D.s.

# 20

# CRITICAL THINKING

*From leading business schools to boards of directors, we see a*
*serious lack of critical thinking and continuous learning.*

Business schools are in their final days of atherosclerosis. Harvard, one of the better business schools, is simply the perfection of the same condition. Most business schools are moving up the wrong alley—at least, that's the response I'm getting from the brightest alumni.

Don't get me wrong. I think my colleagues are terrific—they're doing the best job they can. Still, we need drastic changes. A graduate business school should be based on four foundations:

**1. Critical thinking.** This comes as a consequence of a quality liberal arts education—learning what systemic thinking is all about, how to make connections, how to make sense of the world. Why wouldn't a business school want to offer a course in the great books—on Machiavelli, Hobbes, Hegel, Marx, or Tolstoy? To not read these authors and books is to not understand love, passion, power, and what it means to be human.

**2. Socio-emotional skills.** When I talk to alumni, they say they want more leadership and interpersonal communications skills, writing, communication, presentation of self—this is what our graduates five years out are telling us they lack.

**3. An extended idea family.** Along with "virtual corporations," we need to create "virtual universities." We have the

145

technology to beam in some faculty from Stockholm or Tokyo to create a virtual university or "invisible college"—a group of colleagues, an intellectual community, with whom we can communicate, external to our own universities.

**4. Related work experience.** Consider a model where no student enters graduate school right out of college—only after at least four years of work experience. They're sent and supported by their companies, and they study for no more than a half year and work the rest of the year. So it takes them three or four years to complete a degree.

We need fresh thinking. The quality of the American education system has declined greatly. The K through 12 system is a shambles. Our education system is a receptacle for all our social ills—violence, drugs, debt, broken families. We have a 19th century educational system trying to serve the needs of what will soon be the 21st century. The only answers will come from experimentation and from involvement of parents. We also need creative teachers and administrators who work to involve the parents rather than defend the status quo. We need to examine what we're doing right in our colleges and apply what we can to the K through 12 system. One thing you have at a good university is the sense that you are in a learning environment. We need to build that sense of a learning environment throughout our education system.

### A Lack of Leadership

Like so many things in life, the problem in education isn't money or a lack of caring—the problem is lack of leadership. We must come to a shared vision on education, government, business, industry; we must select good leaders, and we must let them lead.

• **Boards of directors.** Boards of directors might be blamed for not demanding change. But it's hard to put an executive's feet to the fire when he or she is also chairman of the board. Also, it's difficult for board members to move quickly, no matter how brilliant and capable they are.

For example, there are extraordinary people on the boards of IBM and GM. But when you meet only once a month, and you have been appointed by your close friend, I think it takes a while for board members to catch on to what is going on. Not surprisingly, they have a lot of faith in a CEO who's a good person.

To get boards more actively involved sooner in corporate affairs, more companies are moving toward nonexecutive chairmen. We'll see more of that model. Or, we'll see somebody who will be not only chairman of the executive committee but also a senior director, a nonexecutive subchairman of the board. Now, usually the chairman of the board is chairman of the executive committee.

As things are now, the CEO-chairman sets the agenda, and so that's where the power is. That's why I think the CEO and chairman should not be the same person. Had that happened at GM or IBM, we would have seen some changes faster. Boards should be held just as accountable as the CEO. The executive committee could set up some criteria for the board and regularly evaluate its performance. This is where the nonexecutive outside chairman could be useful. To the best of my knowledge, there's no performance evaluation of boards. Boards rarely have a retreat and ask: "Let's look at the way we operate. Are we being level with each other? Taking into account all the data available? Doing a thorough job of evaluating the fiduciary aspects of the business as well as the performance of the CEO?"

That's because some board members are cronies of the CEO and many others are CEOs with too much to do at their own companies. We're getting a new breed of professional director now, but even the professional directors take on too many boards. Right now I serve on four boards, one financial house, and three educational organizations.

As I talk to directors, I detect a feeling from them that the job has become too much. Talk to any of the big executive-search firms and they'll tell you that it's more difficult to get people to serve as directors, especially for banks and firms in financial services. Most board members are, in fact, willing dupes of management—expensive, impotent, and often frustrated, not-so-willing rubber stamps. However, things are changing on that front, as board members fear getting into legal trouble unless they take a greater interest in what's going on.

Most new board members are poorly introduced to the company. Orientation sessions are merely glossy confections that offer little more than the typical annual report. New board members better have the time, interest, and capacity to absorb more sophisticated information. Rarely are new board members oriented so they can understand the company, and they lack the business literacy to evaluate it themselves. Often directors are given a blizzard of paper rather than carefully selected information, and often the information comes a day before the meeting. They may have their own business literacy, but they're being asked to understand another business entirely. That's why new board members need a thorough grounding in the business.

We see a movement to get specific constituencies represented on boards—environmentalists, feminists, minorities. There's a tension between meritocracy and shareholder symmetry in the art of constructing a board. We saw it clearly when Clinton was putting together a Cabinet. At times, his concern with making the Cabinet look like America backfired.

That's not to deny, however, that certain groups are underrepresented as directors, and in the short run it may be necessary to appoint them to boards even if they lack the experience required. But we must be careful. The objective should not be to have the board look like Noah's ark—a black, an environmentalist, a woman, and so on. Then you get people representing constituencies and not the overall organization. That happens because corporations haven't listened to these voices in the past.

Virtually all boards have compensation committees, and these committees should link compensation to performance. All top-management salaries are undergoing stricter scrutiny.

• **Change agent or coach.** The CEO needs somebody to confide in, to talk candidly with about contemplated changes and other important matters. A coach needs to be knowledgeable and nonthreatening and have a sense of history. Several years ago, Jamie Houghton at Corning asked a man named Forrest Behm, a recently retired Corning executive, to be his change agent. For Houghton, Behm served as an alter ego, coach, and sounding board. From him, he got reflective backtalk and feedback.

People in top positions need someone they can talk with openly and honestly. It could be a member of their board; it could be a coach. I'm working now with the head of a Fortune 100 company who wants some coaching on how he can become a better coach. He wants to retire soon and coach the new CEO.

# SECTION THREE

# LEADING CHANGE

Constant change disturbs some managers—it always has, and it always will. Machiavelli said, "Change has no constituency." Well, it better have one—and soon. Forget about regaining global leadership. With only a few short years remaining before the 21st century, we must look now at what it's going to take simply to remain a player in the game. We can do that because the 21st century is with us now. Cultures don't turn sharply with the pages of the calendar—they evolve. By paying attention to what is changing today, we know what we must do better tomorrow.

Can America compete successfully in the new, spirited global economy? If there is reason to despair and join the hand wringing and head shaking of doomsayers, it's because traditional American managers were brought up in a different time, when all they had to do was build the greatest mousetraps and the world beat a path to their doors.

"Leadership in a traditional U.S. company," says R.B. Horton, CEO of BP America, "consisted of creating a management able to cope with competitors who all played with basically the same deck of economic cards." And it was an American game. The competition was fierce but knowable. If you played your cards right, you could win.

But the game has changed: Strange new rules have appeared; the deck has been shuffled; and jokers have been added. Never before has American business faced so many challenges, and never before have there been so many choices about how to face those challenges. Uncertainties and complexities abound. The only thing truly predictable is unpredictability. The new chic is chaos chic. As Yogi Berra put it, "The future ain't what it used to be."

# 21

## CHANGE: THE NEW METAPHYSICS

*Making real progress during change requires true leadership on offense and wise administration on defense.*

Change is the metaphysics of our age. Everything is in motion. Everything mechanical has evolved, become better, more efficient, more sophisticated. In this century, automobiles have advanced from the Model T to the Rolls Royce. Meanwhile, everything organic—from ourselves to tomatoes—has devolved. We have gone from such giants as Teddy Roosevelt, D.W. Griffith, Eugene Debs, Frank Lloyd Wright, Thomas Edison and Albert Michelson to Generation X. Like the new tomatoes, we lack flavor and juice and taste. Manufactured goods are far more impressive than the people who make them. We are less good, less efficient, and less sophisticated with each passing decade.

People in charge have imposed change rather than inspiring it. We have had far more bosses than leaders, and so, finally, everyone has decided to be his or her own boss. This has led to the primitive, litigious, adversarial society we now live in. As the newscaster in the movie "Network" said, "I'm mad as hell, and I'm not going to take it anymore."

What's going on is a middle-class revolution. The poor in America have neither the time nor the energy to revolt. They're just trying to survive in an increasingly hostile world. By the same token, the rich literally reside above the fray—in New York penthouses, Concordes, and sublime ignorance of

151

the world below. The middle class aspires to that same sublime ignorance.

A successful dentist once told me that people become dentists to make a lot of money fast and then go into the restaurant business or real estate, where they will really make money. Young writers and painters are not content to practice their craft and perfect it. Now they want to see and be seen, wheel and deal, and they are as obsessed with the bottom line as are IBM executives. The deal for the publication of a book is far more significant than the book itself, and the cover of *People* magazine is more coveted than a good review in the *New York Times.* The only unions making any noise now are middle-class unions. Professors who once professed an interest in teaching are now far more interested in deals—for the book, the TV appearance, the consulting job, the conference in Paris—leaving teaching to assistants.

When everyone is his or her own boss, no one is in charge, and chaos takes over. Leaders are needed to restore order, by which I mean not obedience but progress. We must begin to use our machines, rather than being used by them. But our least will no longer suffice. It is time for us to control events rather than be controlled by them.

### Avenues of Change

Change occurs in several ways.

• **Dissent and conflict.** We have tried dissent and conflict and have merely become combative. In corporations, change can be mandated by the powers that be. But this leads inevitably to the escalation of rancor. We are perpetually angry now, all walking around with chips on our shoulders. In Los Angeles, people have started shooting each other on the freeways—and sniping at political candidates who shoot themselves down. Our rage seems both mindless and endless.

• **Trust and truth.** Positive change requires trust, clarity and participation. At this juncture, all three seem as distant as Jupiter. But we have reached Jupiter, and so perhaps we can finally reach ourselves. Only people with virtue and vision can lead us out of this bog and back to the high ground, doing three things: 1) gaining our trust; 2) expressing their vision clearly so that we all not only understand but concur; and 3) persuading us to participate.

• **Cliques and cabals.** The cliques have the power, the money and the resources. The cabals, usually younger and always ambitious, have drive and energy. Unless the cliques can co-opt the cabals, revolution is inevitable. This avenue, too, is messy. It can lead to either a stalemate or an ultimate victory for the cabals, if for no other reason than that they have staying power.

• **External events.** Forces of society can impose themselves on the organization. For example, the auto industry was forced to change its ways and its products, both by government regulation and by foreign competition. In the same way, student activists forced many universities to rewrite their curricula and add black studies and women's studies programs. Academicians are still debating both the sense and the efficacy of such programs, as they have altered not only what students learn but how they learn it.

• **Culture or paradigm shift.** The most important avenue of change is culture or paradigm. In *The Structure of Scientific Revolution,* Thomas Kuhn notes that the paradigm in science is akin to a zeitgeist or climate of opinion that governs choices. He defines it as "the constellation of values and beliefs shared by the members of a scientific community that determines the choice, problems which are regarded as significant, and the approaches to be adopted in attempting to solve it." According to Kuhn, the people who have revolutionized science have always been those who have changed the paradigm.

• **Innovators and leaders.** People who change not merely the content of a particular discipline but its practice and focus are not only innovators but leaders. Ralph Nader, who refocused the legal profession to address consumer problems, was such a person. Betty Friedan, in truthfully defining how women lived, inspired them to live in different ways. Freud, Keynes, and Gropius, each in his own field, created new metaphors of practice that were valid and compelling.

It is not the articulation of a profession or organization's goals that creates new practices but rather the imagery that creates the understanding, the compelling moral necessity for the new way. The clarity of the metaphor and the energy and courage its maker brings to it are vital to its acceptance. For example, when Branch Rickey, general manager of the

Brooklyn Dodgers, decided to bring black players into professional baseball, he chose Jackie Robinson, a paragon among players and among men.

How do we identify and develop such innovators? How do we spot new information in institutions, organizations and professions? Innovators, like all creative people, see things differently, think in fresh and original ways. They have useful contacts in other areas, other institutions; they are seldom seen as good organization men or women and often viewed as mischievous troublemakers. The true leader not only is an innovator but makes every effort to locate and use other innovators in the organization. He or she creates a climate in which conventional wisdom can be questioned and challenged and one in which errors are embraced rather than shunned in favor of safe, low-risk goals.

In organizations, people have norms, values, shared beliefs, and paradigms of what is right and what is wrong, what is legitimate and what is not, and how things are done. One gains status and power through agreement, concurrence, and conformity with these paradigms. Therefore, both dissent and innovation are discouraged. Every social system contains these forces for conservatism, for maintaining the status quo at any cost, but it must also contain means for movement, or it will eventually become paralyzed.

Basic changes take place slowly because those with power typically have no knowledge, and those with knowledge have no power. Anyone with real knowledge of history and the world as it is today could redesign society and develop a new paradigm in an afternoon, but turning theory into fact could take a lifetime—unless the person happened to be president of the United States.

Still, we have to try because too many of our organizations and citizens are locked into roles and practices that simply do not work. True leaders work to gain the trust of their constituents, communicate their vision lucidly, and thus involve everyone in the process of change. They then try to use the inevitable dissent and conflict creatively and positively, and out of all that, sometimes, a new paradigm emerges.

A Harris poll showed that over 90 percent of the people polled would change their lives dramatically if they could, and they ranked such intangibles as self-respect, affection, and acceptance higher than status, money, and power. They don't like the way they live now, but they don't know how to change. The poll is evidence of our need for real leaders and should serve as impetus and inspiration to potential leaders and innovators. If such people have the will to live up to their potential—and the rest of us have the gumption to follow them—we might finally find our way out of this bog we're in.

### Avoiding Disaster During Change

Constant as change has been and vital as it is now, it is still hard to effect, because the sociology of institutions is fundamentally antichange. Here, then, are ten ways to avoid disaster during periods of change—any time, all the time—except in those organizations that are dying or dead.

**1. Recruit with scrupulous honesty.** Enthusiasm or plain need often inspires recruiters to transmogrify visible and real drawbacks and make them reappear as exhilarating challenges. Recruiting is, after all, a kind of courtship ritual. The suitor displays his or her assets and masks his or her defects. The recruit, flattered by the attention and the promises, does not examine the proposal thoughtfully. He or she looks forward to opportunities to be truly creative and imaginative and to support from the top. Inadvertently, the recruiter has cooked up the classic recipe for revolution as suggested by Aaron Wildavsky: "Promise a lot; deliver a little. Teach people to believe they will be much better off, but let there be no dramatic improvement. Try a variety of small programs but marginal in impact and severely underfinanced. Avoid any attempted solution remotely comparable in size to the dimensions of the problem you're trying to solve."

When expectations are too high and promises too grand, disillusionment is inevitable. The disparity between vision and reality becomes intolerable.

**2. Guard against the crazies.** Innovation is seductive. It attracts interesting people. It also attracts people who will distort your ideas into something monstrous. You will then be identified with the monster and be forced to spend precious energy combating it. A change-oriented administrator should be damned sure that the people he or she recruits are change agents but not agitators. It is difficult sometimes to tell the difference between the innovators and the crazies. Eccentricities and idiosyncrasies in change agents are often useful and valuable. Neurosis isn't.

**3. Build support among like-minded people, whether or not you recruited them.** Change-oriented administrators are particularly prone to act as though the organization came into being the day they arrived. This is a delusion, a fantasy of omnipotence. There are no clean slates in established organizations. A new CEO can't play Noah and build the world anew with a handpicked crew of his or her own. Rhetoric about new starts is frightening to those who sense that this new beginning is the end of their careers. There can be no change without history and continuity. In addition, some of the old hands have, besides knowledge and experience, real creativity. A clean sweep, then, is often a waste of resources.

**4. Plan for change from a solid conceptual base.** Have a clear understanding of how to change as well as what to change. Planning changes is always easier than implementing them. If change is to be permanent, it must be gradual. Incremental reform can be successful by drawing on a rotating nucleus of people who continually read the data provided by the organization and the society in which it operates for clues that it's time to adapt. Without such critical nuclei, organizations cannot be assured of continued self-renewal. Such people must not be faddists but must be hypersensitive to ideas whose hour has come. They must also know when ideas are antithetical to the organization's purposes and values and when they will enhance and strengthen the organization.

**5. Don't settle for rhetorical change.** Significant change cannot simply be decreed. Any organization has two structures: one on paper and another that consists of a complex set of intramural relationships. A good administrator understands the relationships and creates a good fit between them and any planned alterations. Those who get caught up in their own rhetoric almost inevitably neglect the demanding task of maintaining established constituencies and building new ones.

**6. Don't allow those who are opposed to change to appropriate basic issues.** Successful change agents make sure that respectable people are not afraid of what is to come and that the old guard isn't frightened at the prospect of change. The moment such people get scared is the moment they begin to fight dirty. They not only have some built-in clout, they have tradition on their side.

**7. Know the territory.** Learn everything there is to know about the organization and about its locale, which often means mastering the politics of local chauvinism, along with an intelligent public relations program. In Southern California, big developers are constantly being blindsided by neighborhood groups because they have not bothered to acquaint the groups with their plans. The neighborhood groups often triumph, too, forcing big changes or cancellations in the planned development. They know their rights and they know the law, and the developers haven't made the effort to know them.

**8. Appreciate environmental factors.** No matter how laudable or profitable or imaginative, a change that increases discomfort in the organization is probably doomed. Adding a sophisticated new computer system is probably a good thing, but it can instantly be seen as a bad thing if it results in overcrowded offices.

**9. Avoid future shock.** When an executive becomes too involved in planning, he or she frequently forgets the past and neglects the present. As a result, before the plan goes into effect, employees are probably already opposed to it. They, after all, have to function in the here and now, and if their boss's eye is always on tomorrow, he or she is not giving them the attention and support they need. Furthermore, when an organization focuses too much on a vision of future greatness, everyone is bound to be disillusioned with the reality.

**10. Remember that change is most successful when those who are affected are involved in the planning.** This is a platitude of planning theory, but it is as true as it is trite. Nothing makes people resist new ideas or approaches more adamantly than their belief that change is being imposed on them.

The problems connected with innovation and change are common to every modern bureaucracy. University, government and corporation all respond similarly to challenge and to crisis, with much the same explicit or implicit codes, punctilios and mystiques.

Means must be found to stimulate the pursuit of truth—that is, the true nature of the organization's problems—in an open and democratic way. This calls for classic means: an examined life, a spirit of inquiry and genuine experimentation, a life based on discovering new realities, taking risks, suffering occasional defeats, and not fearing the surprises of the future. The model for truly innovative organizations in an era of constant change is the scientific model. As scientists seek and discover truths, so organizations must seek and discover their own truths—that carefully, that thoroughly, that honestly, that imaginatively, and that courageously.

# 22

## INTRODUCING CHANGE

*Every leader needs a flight plan since leading means*
*doing the right things, and managing means doing things right.*

Leaders often face the challenge of introducing change to those who simply see no need for it. From my research on effective leaders, there are certain steps a leader must take to bring about such a change effectively.

For example, school administrators have the tough role of being change agents and leaders in a challenging environment. They must work within a system populated by noisy, eloquent stakeholders who are continually scrutinizing every action—a system that can be best characterized with the oxymoron "an organized anarchy," because most of the individuals in a school system have much education and are highly individualistic.

### Vision and Mission

The question ultimately becomes: How does a leader rally individuals—from different disciplines and different areas of expertise—behind an overarching and compelling vision?

The first thing all leaders must do, regardless of whether they are leading General Motors or IBM or a school system, is to clearly articulate a vision. Whether the leader calls it a strategic intent, mission, conviction, set of beliefs, or vision, it must be communicated clearly, compellingly, forcibly, and simply. And it isn't enough to talk generally about strategic goals or objectives. A vision must be communicated ceaselessly, indefatigably, and endlessly in all sorts of ways. It isn't enough to do it through memos, newsletters, or satellite broadcasts. Most of the communication must be done eyeball to eyeball. In addition, that vision must be anchored in realities.

Most organizations have terrific vision statements. Companies are great at printing mission statements on three-by-five laminated plaques along with elaborate lists of company visions and values. Dazzling documents like this are useless.

I once consulted for a large utilities firm in Southern California which had a wonderful vision statement called the "Six Commitments." These commitments hung on the wall of every office. But not one of them was anchored in reality, and not one of them was implemented. For example, one commitment was, "We believe in the autonomy of the worker and in self-managed work teams and in empowerment." But in that company you would have to get six signatures to take a 25-mile trip away from the office.

Another company stated, "We believe in teamwork," and yet there was an implicit norm that one never brought to the surface conflict or dissent or disagreement. Well, how can you create teamwork when you never bring to the surface differences, healthy dissent, and creative conflict?

Executives must not just articulate a simple and compelling vision, but they must take this vision into account when doing everything that they do—when thinking about recruiting and reward systems, when considering empowerment, when changing the structure, when pursuing new markets, and when making decisions.

The only way a leader is going to translate vision into reality—an ability that is the essence of leadership—is to anchor and implement and execute that vision through a variety of policies, practices, procedures, and systems that will bring in people and empower them to implement the vision.

Leaders must also discover the individuals who are "variance sensors," who expect things beyond the current reality, who see the need for change, and who have the future in their bones.

I view any change as a three-act play. Act One is creating the vision. Act Two is changing the system and implementing it. Act Three is stabilizing and putting into effect those system changes that went on in the second act.

This idea is similar to the old paradigm that Kurt Lewen talked about many years ago regarding the three acts of changing. He said that the first act is to "unfreeze"; the second act is to "start changing"; and the third act is to "refreeze." And this cycle must be continual. After the freeze, unfreeze again; keep changing and keep refreezing.

I used to think that running an organization was equivalent to conducting a symphony orchestra. But I don't think that's quite it; it's more like jazz. There is more improvisation. Someone once wrote that the sound of surprise is jazz, and if there's any one thing that we must try to get used to in this world, it's surprise and the unexpected. Truly, we are living in a world where the only thing that's constant is change.

Leaders must create an environment that embraces change not as a threat but as an opportunity. That requires leaders to listen to—and act on—the multiple sounds around them. Leaders must encourage their organizations to dance to forms of music yet to be heard.

The leader's role is to impart a sense of vision, purpose, strategic intent, mission. A leader must embody a powerful distillation of an organization's purpose and objectives. Management, on the other hand, is more concerned with doing things right—with efficiency, with control mechanisms and the short run.

Essentially, the manager administers and the leader innovates. The manager is a copy; the leader is an original. The manager maintains; the leader develops. The manager accepts the status quo; the leader is always questioning and challenging the gospel. The manager focuses on the systems and structure; the leader focuses on people. The manager relies on the control; the leader inspires trust. The manager has a short-range view; the leader has a long-range perspective. The manager imitates; the leader originates.

The manager asks "how" and "when," and the leader asks "what" and "why." Effective leaders do not tell their subordinates "how." Instead leaders try to create a tapestry of intentions.

### Over-Managed and Under-Led

Today's organizations are over-managed and under-led. They are overly concerned with policies, practices, procedures, and rule books and not concerned enough with the important issues like empowerment, trust, mission, and an overarching and compelling vision. Basically, leadership is all about translating intention and vision into reality. Leaders keep their eyes on the horizon, not just on the bottom line.

In times of rapid change, there is no substitute for leadership. Unfortunately, most organizations are based on an old-fashioned form of bureaucracy, the mind-set of control, order, and predict. Those are the things of management. If we existed in an environment where we could control, order, and predict, a manager would be a terrific thing. Bureaucracy in a stable environment, as it was in the Victorian era, would be a great social invention.

But today, organizations are unhinged. They are confusing and full of surprises. We are all children of chaos. And so we must develop and educate leaders who originate, innovate, and have the imagination to see what the future will be like.

A problem with organizations such as IBM, Sears, Westinghouse, and Eastman Kodak is that their leaders were so immersed in details, with trivia—with "administrivia"—and with the "how-to" that they forgot what's important. For example, IBM used to have a plant in Kentucky that was losing money because it was manufacturing typewriters. So they spent a half-billion dollars to reengineer the plant to make printers. But they were making the wrong printers because they didn't see the potential in the laser printer. And in a few months, they were surpassed by Hewlett-Packard and Apple. It's an example of doing things right, but doing the wrong things.

### Portrait of a Leader

Leaders have certain traits in common.

• **First, they have a great deal of self-knowledge.** They have a strong sense of who they are as human beings. Leadership is character, and character is knowing one's ingredients.

• **Second, they have a strongly defined sense of purpose.** Achieving, successful leaders know what is important. And they always are reminding people of what's important. It's not enough to just have vision; it's not enough to just know your objectives. Instead, a leader must create an environment where people are aware of why they are there. You can see this even in a university. Occasionally when we will gather in the faculty club and talk, someone will say—always in jest to conceal the basic truth—"wouldn't this be a good place to be if only there weren't students around." Well, why are we there? Why are we administrating school systems and universities? Primarily we are there to help educate students to be successful in life. Everything else is a cost factor or a commentary.

• **Third, leaders have the capacity to generate and sustain trust.** And the way they tend to do this is by being candid, by communicating effectively and by exhibiting a sense of constancy and caring. If leaders can somehow communicate and in that communication show that they care, show that they're candid and indicate their competence, then they will generate and sustain trust.

• **Fourth, leaders have a bias toward action.** It makes no sense to be in the dugout or kibitzing from the bleachers. Leaders are at bat. They play even if it means making errors. And when they make errors, they learn from their errors.

### Learning About Leadership

The most dangerous leadership myth is that leaders are born—that there is a genetic factor to leadership. This myth asserts that people simply either have certain charismatic qualities or not. That's nonsense; in fact, the opposite is true. Leaders are made rather than born. And the way we become leaders is by learning about leadership through life and job experiences, not with university degrees.

Leadership is nurtured with on-the-job education through role models. People learn to be leaders through difficult experiences and when they face adversity. They learn through the pain and agony of having to come up with the hard answers. In some cases, being fired was the learning experience leaders looked back on as a focus of their leadership training; in other cases it was having to downsize. In one case it was having to take over an inexperienced group of subordinates. But ultimately, the only way people learn about leadership is by being placed into situations from which they can learn and get feedback from valued sources around them.

Leadership doesn't come from genes. It doesn't come from reading or listening to lectures. It comes through the hard-earned experience in the arena rather than watching from the balcony.

# 23

## CHANGE AGENTS

*The role of the innovative change agent involves risks, but these can be managed using competence and value power.*

While change agents are not a very homogeneous group, they do have some similarities. Among them are the following four:

• **Their assumptions.** They take for granted the centrality of work to men and women employed in highly organized settings. They are concerned with organizational effectiveness, improvement, development, and enhancement. While their prescriptions vary, their diagnosis of organizational health pivots on interpersonal or group relationships and the implications of these on changes in technology, structure, and tasks. Although they are aware of these three nonpersonal factors and occasionally focus on them, their main preoccupation is with people and the processes of human interaction. They are not interested in changing (or transferring) personnel but in the relationships, attitudes, perceptions, and values of existing personnel.

• **Their roles.** They may play a variety of roles to bring about innovative change: researchers, trainers, consultants, counselors, teachers, and, in some cases, line managers. Some change agents specialize in one role, but most shift and switch from one to another. Frequently, change agents are not actual members of the client system. Some say that significant change depends on the impetus generated by an external agent. They argue that only a skilled outside consultant can provide the perspective, detachment, and energy necessary to alter existing patterns. Advocates of the internal consultant take the opposite stand. They argue that the insider possesses the intimate knowledge of the client system (and the power to legitimize) that the external change agent lacks. In addition, the internal change agent does not generate the suspicion and mistrust that the outsider often does. Their acceptance and credibility are often guaranteed by organizational status. Change agents tend to be self-conscious about their roles and their role changes vis-à-vis their clients.

• **Their interventions.** Change agents intervene at different levels and at different times. For example, they may intervene with discrepancy, calling attention to a contradiction in action or attitudes; theory, citing research findings or adding conceptual understanding to help people gain perspective; procedure, offering a critique of existing methods for solving problems; relationships, focusing on tensions growing out of interpersonal relationships; experimentation, setting up comparisons and testing actions before making a decision; dilemma, identifying significant choice points or exigencies in problem solving, trying to understand assumptions, and searching for alternatives; perspective, providing situational and historical understanding of problems; structure, identifying the source of problems as bound in the structure and systems; and cultural, examining traditions.

• **Their values and goals.** Their goals, although stated with varying clarity and specificity, imply a particular vision of people and organization and a particular set of values that form the base for this vision. Their values are aroused by dissatisfaction with the ineffectiveness of bureaucratic organizations. Though each change agent has a unique set of values and goals, most change agents would agree to some general aims. For example, they oppose bureaucratic values that are impersonal and task-oriented and lead to poor, shallow, mistrustful, nonauthentic relationships that tend to be "phony," unhelpful, and incomplete and block the natural and free expression of feelings, leading to a state of decreased interpersonal competence. Without effective interpersonal competence among management, an organization is a breeding ground for mistrust, intergroup conflict, and rigidity, which in turn lead to a decrease in whatever criteria the organization is using to measure its effectiveness.

Bureaucratic values stress the rational, task aspects of work and ignore the human factors. Managers who come up under this system of values are badly cast to play the intricate human roles now required of them. Their ineptitude and anxieties lead to systems of discord and defense and interfere with problem solving.

### Realities of the Role

The change agent's role must be construed as being professional, marginal, ambiguous, insecure, and risky.

• **Professional.** Change agents count heavily on a body of certified knowledge to realize their aims, under guidance of certain ethical principles, and with the client's interest—not their own—in mind. Change agents must defer their own personal gratification in their dealings with the client system. When working with large and complex organizations—where their actions may affect thousands of people—they must continually check their own needs, motives, and wishes against the reality of the client's needs.

• **Marginal.** Change agents rarely have formal membership in the client system or a band of colleagues working close by. Typically they work alone, and their marginality can work to their advantage and to their discomfort. On the positive side, the marginality can enhance their detachment and perception; it can also create insecurity and an absence of mechanisms (like colleagues) for reality testing. In any case, both the target system and the change agent have to come to terms with the marginality.

• **Ambiguous.** The change agent is not widely understood. The ambiguity of the role betrays its lack of legitimacy and credibility. It also involves certain risks, such as drawing suspicion and hostility. But it can also be helpful in providing the necessary latitude and breadth which more precisely defined roles do not allow.

• **Insecure.** Insecurity stems from a precarious employment base (the fact that the change agent may be the most expendable person under certain conditions); inadequate knowledge and a lack of guidelines for many actions; and profound resistance, which develops when one attempts to change an organization.

- **Risky.** The risk is not only to the target system but also to the agent's professional status. The complexity of organizational change and some of its unanticipated consequences can lead to totally undesirable outcomes.

### Required Competencies

To achieve success, change agents need to possess four competencies:

- **Broad knowledge.** Their intellect must encompass a wide range of knowledge, including conceptual-diagnostic knowledge, cutting across the entire sector of the behavioral sciences, theories, and methods of change; knowledge of sources of help; and orientation to the ethical and evaluative functions of the role.

- **Operational and relational skills.** Change agents must also possess operational and relational skills—the ability to listen, observe, identify, and report; to form relationships and inspire trust; and to manifest a high degree of behavioral flexibility.

- **Sensitive and mature.** Change agents must also be in constant communication with themselves and recognize and come to grips with their own motivations. In the diagnostic stages, change agents must observe how the target system deals with them. Often, the interaction between change agents and the target system is crucial for understanding the state and readiness of the target system.

- **Authenticity.** Change agents must act congruently and authentically in accordance with the values they attempt to superimpose on the target system. It will not do for the change-agent to impose democratic or humanistic values in an authoritarian or inhuman manner. If the change agent is concerned with creating more authenticity and collaboration, he or she must behave in ways that are in accord with these values—not only for the obvious ethical reasons but for deeper reasons as well. So much of the change agent's influence grows out of his or her relationship with the target system and the extent to which the change agent is emulated as a role model that any significant discrepancies between his or her actions and stated values cannot help but create resistance.

These requirements of the change agent's role sound almost saintly. We should not expect to find many such saints among us, but we might use this job description as something to aim for.

### Sources of Power

What power sources do change agents tap to exert their influence? Power is the ability to influence, and power is derived from at least five sources:

• **Coercive power.** This refers to the ability to reward or punish. Change agents typically don't possess the means to exert coercive power because they are external to the organization and do not hold any formal title. Moreover, most change agents would prefer, at least intellectually, not to wield coercive power, whether or not they possess it, for at least two reasons: first, coercive power appears to be at variance with their normative goals and values; and second, coercive power is not as durable, except under conditions of vigilant surveillance.

• **Referent or identification power.** This refers to the influence that accrues to A because he or she (or the group) is attractive, a person whom B wants to like and be liked by—in short, a role model. Most change agents will use some referent power and attribute some amount of their influence to the client system's ability and desire to emulate them.

• **Expert power.** This is the power that we associate with science and truth. Change agents may use some expert power, but they are not always perceived as a source of really "useful" knowledge. True, in varying degrees, they possess useful information about the human side of the enterprise. But this knowledge is rarely considered "expert" enough—in the sense that an engineer, doctor, lawyer is seen as a source of expertise.

• **Legitimate or traditional power.** This power stems from institutional norms and practices and from historical-legal traditions. Change agents will likely not use traditional power because they continually work without legitimization. Often, they are perceived as odd men out, as strangers, as marginal to the enterprise.

• **Value power.** This influence is gained on the basis of attraction to values. Change agents tap this source of power most. They influence others by representing and transmitting values that are admired and desired by the client system. Most change agents embody a set of values and communicate them to the client system verbally or otherwise, emitting cues that provide a consistent value system: concern for our fellow man, experimentalism, openness, honesty, flexibility, cooperation, and democracy. This set of values seems to be extremely potent in influencing top management circles.

These values indicate a certain way of behaving and feeling. They emphasize openness rather than secrecy, superior-subordinate collaboration rather than dependence or rebellion, cooperation rather than competition, consensus rather than individual rule, rewards based on self-control rather than externally induced rewards, team leadership rather than a one-to-one relationship with the boss, and authentic relationships rather than those based on political maneuverings.

# 24

# TOO MANY CHIEFS

*Organizations having both a CEO and a COO
can often attest: two chiefs may be one too many.*

In the beginning, organizations were exceedingly simple. There were chiefs and tribes, or kings and subjects, or owners and tenants, or bosses and workers.

With the advent of the Industrial Revolution, things got more complicated. There were stockholders, boards of directors, officers and employees. Now it's too complicated—with stakeholders and shareholders, chairmen of the boards and CEOs, corporate presidents and COOs, assorted vice presidents, managers and employees. Naturally, the modern organization, being complicated, even Byzantine, is much more subject to trouble, or even breakdowns, than its predecessors.

### A Classic Example
As a rule, such organizational breakdowns occur in the privacy of corporate executive suites, but the whole world witnessed a classic example of structural failure during the White House power struggle that climaxed with President Ronald Reagan firing his chief of staff, Donald Regan.

The president was rapped for this "managerial style," but actually the problems resided in his managerial mode. Reagan and Regan learned the hard way that there are more weaknesses than strengths in the two-track CEO-COO mode.

Given its political bias, the Reagan administration's choice of a corporate structure over a bureaucratic chain of command was reasonable, as was the appointment of Regan, a top business executive, as chief of staff. But Regan's view of his role was anything but reasonable, and became the basis for the subsequent firestorm.

Though Chief of Staff Regan was the White House equivalent of a COO serving CEO Reagan, from the outset he behaved like a CEO, usurping both Reagan's authority and prerogatives. COOs are secondary, not primary spokespersons, yet Regan issued frequent off-the-cuff pronouncements, which were often at odds with his boss's policies and pronouncements. Furthermore, COO Regan isolated CEO Reagan from both his staff and his constituents, which resulted in the CEO seeing the world more and more through his COO's lens.

Finally, of course, the flaws in the two men's relationship magnified the flaws inherent in the structure and brought it all down. Regan, the quintessential corporate boss, was replaced by Howard Baker, the quintessential bureaucratic team player.

As something like order returned to the White House, Iran and Contragate notwithstanding, there must have been sympathetic sighs and nods in corporate headquarters all over America, because no one knows how flawed and how basically unworkable the CEO-COO power split is than the CEOs and COOs themselves.

Contemporary corporate structure is, at best, a jerry-built rig, which emerged out of perceived need and chance, rather than choice. And like every fragile, sensitive machine, it's only as good as its parts.

The principal parts of the corporate machine are people, and people come to the job at hand with all their own sensitivities, fragilities and needs. The higher a person rises in the corporate hierarchy, the more exposed his strengths and weaknesses are, and nowhere are these strengths and weaknesses more exposed and more tested than in the relationship between a CEO and his COO.

On paper, the differences between the two jobs are very clear. The CEO is the leader, the COO the manager. The CEO is charged with doing the right thing, the COO with doing things right. The CEO takes the long view, the COO the short view. The CEO concentrates on the what and why, while the COO focuses on how. The CEO has the vision, the COO hands-on control. The CEO thinks in terms of innovations, development, the future, while the COO is busy with administration, maintenance, the present. The CEO sets the tone and direction, both inside and outside the company, while the COO sets the pace.

Ironically, as with Reagan and Regan, even when the CEO and COO function happily together, they can run into big trouble, as mutual admiration is not necessarily relevant, much less productive. But when they're unhappy together, their unhappiness is reflected throughout the organization in major and minor ways, which leads to trouble, too.

### One Head Better Than Two

No one makes it into the upper reaches of the corporate world without a very healthy ego and very strong opinions about everything. Given this, even the most serene CEO (which may be an oxymoron) is bound to occasionally envy the COO's hands-on control, while the COO must long sometimes to think ahead, dream, innovate. The logic here is that two heads are better than one, but I don't know any top executives who, in their heart of hearts, don't think that their own head is better than all the other heads put together.

In addition to these fundamental problems, there are other traps in the structure. What the CEO imagines, the COO makes manifest—often in ways that seem wrong to the CEO. Then, too, the COO seems the natural heir to the CEO, and if there were any real sense in this structure, he or she would be. But COO skills, which are primarily managerial, are not necessarily useful in the CEO slot, which requires leader's talents. And so superb managers can move into the leader's chair and find themselves back at square one, scrambling to learn a whole new game, and often striking out.

If the COO opposes his CEO, no matter how valid his position, one time or twenty times, he may jeopardize his ultimate ascension. This may serve to intimidate or inhibit, making him both a less effective COO and a less likely CEO candidate.

Obviously, any COO comes to the job with his own managerial style, and, if he's any good at all, he has both knowledge of and ideas about his company and the desire to use his knowledge to the full and express his ideas freely. But, if the COO doesn't see eye to eye with his CEO, he can either challenge the CEO or remain silent. If the COO challenges the CEO, he may, depending on both the wisdom of the challenge and the character of the CEO, risk incurring the enmity of the CEO, which means his days are probably numbered as COO and the chances of ever getting the top job are nil.

On the other hand, if the COO remains silent, then he does both himself and the company a disservice. The moment any executive begins to tailor his ideas and performance to suit the boss, he is diminished, and, because no CEO is infallible, the company may lose, too. In addition, any time a COO, or any other top executive, deliberately trims the sails, withholding ideas or energy from the company, he simultaneously reduces his own opportunities for advancement.

Don Regan's downfall was a direct result of his assuming too much authority and too little responsibility. He spoke too much for the president and too little to him, withholding any ideas or information which were at odds with his own. If he had been less a censor and more of a critic, Regan might still be in the White House.

The COO is, then, constantly between a rock and a hard place, damned if he does and damned if he doesn't. The COO's first loyalty must always be to the company. It, after all, pays him very well and expects the COO to give 100 percent on the job. But if he gives 100 percent, applying all his knowledge, experience and expertise, the COO may find himself on the outs with the CEO who, for good reason or no reason at all, feels threatened by his second-in-command.

### An Unworkable Structure?

The two-track CEO-COO structure is so susceptible to problems because, at bottom, it's unworkable. However clean and clear the division of responsibilities is on paper, in practice these responsibilities are indivisible, inextricably interwoven. Every leader has something of the manager in him, and every top manager has qualities of leadership—or he probably wouldn't have made it to the top. Thus, the CEO wears both leadership and managerial hats, and is bound to tread on the COO's turf at least occasionally. At the same time, the COO can't resist flexing his leadership muscles occasionally, and assuming some of the CEO's prerogatives.

In the same line, the conscientious COO wants not merely to do things right, but to do the right thing, and wants, too, to occasionally take the long view. Indeed, it is impossible not to take the long view sometimes.

The solution to the CEO-COO dilemma is as simple as the structure is complex. The key responsibilities of both the CEO and COO should be combined and assigned to a CEO-in-chief, who would reside at the center of a constellation of executives.

This CEO-in-chief would be the leader and the manager of managers, each of whom would superintend a portion of the company's operations. He would be expected to do the right thing, enabling his managers to do things right. He would be responsible for seeing that the short view was compatible with the long view, that things done today would lead to tomorrow's goals. The CEO-in-chief would define the whats and whys and assign the hows to associates.

The CEO-in-chief would have the vision and primary hands-on control, thus insuring that his vision was always realistic. He would think in terms of innovation, development, and the future, while his associates took care of administration, maintenance and the present, and he would set tone, direction and pace. Since the division of these various tasks was arbitrary, even accidental, their reunion would make for a generally more effective, efficient operation, along with eliminating the possibility of CEO-COO conflicts.

Since the CEO-in-chief's assistants would possess both the requisite managerial and leadership skills and talents and would gain broad experience working with and for their CEO, some would be likely candidates for the top spot. The CEO-in-chief would be limited to a seven-year term—to insure against burnout, complacency or any of the other afflictions CEOs are now heir to.

With less structure and more leadership, American business might begin to recover its verve, energy and spunk.

# 25

## From CEO to CTO

*Even successful organizations may undo themselves in the future
if they continue to act today the way they acted in the past.*

The CEO must become the Chief Transformation Officer
or CTO. The very culture of the organization must change
because, as constituted, that culture is probably more devoted
to preserving itself than to meeting new challenges.

Transforming culture poses a formidable task. As Robert
Haas, Chairman and CEO of Levi Strauss & Co., says:

> *It's difficult to unlearn behaviors that made us suc-
> cessful in the past—speaking rather than listening;
> valuing people like yourself over people of different gen-
> ders or from different cultures; doing things on your
> own rather than collaborating; making the decision
> yourself instead of asking different people for their per-
> spectives. There's a whole range of behaviors that were
> highly functional in the hierarchical organization that
> are dead wrong in the flatter, more responsive, empow-
> ered organization that we're seeking to become.*

Management is getting people to do what needs to be done.
Leadership is getting people to want to do what needs to be
done. Managers push. Leaders pull. Managers command.
Leaders communicate.

Effective leaders align, create, and empower. Leaders need
to align the resources to create a sense of shared vision and

objectives worthy of support, even dedication. When resources are aligned around a shared vision, people tend to have high aspirations. Work becomes part of pursuing a larger purpose embodied in the organization's products and services.

Effective leaders create adaptive, creative, learning organizations where problems are identified before they become crises and where resources are rallied to solve the problems. They test possible solutions, perhaps by means of a pilot program, and they reflect on and evaluate past actions and decisions.

When empowered, people sense that they are at the center of things rather than on the periphery. When organizations are effectively led, everyone feels he or she contributes to their success. Empowered individuals believe that their actions have significance and meaning. Empowered people have discretion, but also obligations. They live in a culture of respect, trust, and system-wide communication where they can do things without getting permission from some parent figure.

Whatever shape the future takes, successful organizations must take seriously—and sustain through action—the belief that their competitive advantage is based on the development and growth of the people in them. The men and women who guide those organizations will be different leaders than the ones we've become used to. They will be maestros, not masters; coaches, not commanders.

Challenging the status quo, especially when you have been successful, is difficult to do. Roberto Goizueta, CEO of Coca-Cola, once told his managers:

> *If you think you are going to be successful running your business in the next ten years the way you did the last ten years, you're out of your mind. In order to succeed, we have to disturb the present.*

Tumultuous change is driven by technology, globalization and demographic diversity. These forces have profound effects not only on how businesses operate, but on how people conduct their lives.

Almost all organizations are caught between two paradigms in how they are organized and how they are led. On the one hand, we have bureaucracy with the mind-set of control, order, and predict and with clear lines of distinction and no cross-functional work modes. But today we have eloquent stakeholders whose voices have to be taken into account. Today, we are moving toward organizations formed more like temporary systems, networks, or clusters. Their mind-set will be alignment, creativity, and empowerment.

In the post-bureaucratic world, the laurel will go to the leader who encourages healthy dissent and values followers brave enough to say no. Successful leaders will have, not the loudest voice, but the readiest ear. And their genius may well lie not in personal achievements, but in unleashing other people's talent.

### Three Observations

When I set out to see if all effective leaders are alike, I observed and interviewed hundreds of leaders, their direct reports, and some family and board members.

Reflecting on this experience, I make three observations:
• Leadership is the key determinant in the success or failure of any human institution.
• Effective leadership must be related to the times in which it functions.
• Almost all organizations are presently caught between two paradigms in how they organize themselves and how they are led.

Jack Welch, Chairman and CEO of General Electric, has correctly predicted:

> The future will not belong to managers or to those who make the numbers dance, or to those who are conversant with all the jargon we use to sound smart. The world will belong to passionate, driven leaders—people who not only have an enormous energy, but who can energize those whom they lead.

The stock price of publicly held organizations is determined largely by the perception of quality in the leadership at the top. Beyond stock price, the leader also sets the tone for the moral character, vision, culture, and the fiber of the institution.

While one school of thought believes leaders are created by the events in their lives, I believe that the character of the leaders makes the difference. The Tolstoyans talk about leadership as surfing: A good leader catches the wave at the right time and manages to ride in with it. I say that great leaders make waves. All history is biography and great institutions are the direct reflection of the leaders who create them.

Leadership has to do with vision, mission, strategic intent, dreams. Managers are more involved in the how-to, the short-term, the bottom line—factors referred to as the "hard side" of management. In the past, the hard side of business meant getting the goods out the door, while the "soft side" meant the values of the workforce. However, the distinction between hard and soft is disappearing. You won't get the goods out the door without taking the values of the workforce very seriously.

### Prime Characteristics

Future leaders must have three characteristics—a deep sense of purpose, trust, and optimism—as well as character. Of the six criteria commonly used to choose leaders—technical competence, people skills, conceptual skills, judgment, taste, and character—the most important considerations are the latter three. In fact, the last, character, will make or break a leader.

• **Purpose.** The first critical ingredient in character is purpose, a willful determination to get what leaders want. The derivative of purpose is results. Purpose is the central ingredient of power. Powerful people and organizations have a strong, sometimes even skewed, sense of purpose. Michael Eisner, CEO of The Walt Disney Company, told me recently he believed that "point of view" was very important, and noted that in his organization someone with a strong point of view always wins the day. I see this as an expression of purpose. Eisner said, "Around here, a strong point of view is worth eighty IQ points."

• **Trust.** The second key attribute of a strong character is trust, especially in these times of roiling change when it seems difficult to trust anyone. Building trust in organizations depends on the four "Cs": caring, constancy, competence, and congruity. One of the things you hear about ineffective leaders is that they act on the recommendations of the last person they spoke to—they have no sense of constancy, competence, or congruity. The reason great leaders are effective is because they have congruity of character. They are people whose vision and beliefs are congruent with what they feel and what they say and do.

Leaders generate and sustain trust. Under the umbrella of

trust are such traits as competence, caring, constancy, reliability, predictability, and integrity. What leaders think, feel and do are like concentric circles. That's why it drives people crazy when leaders don't walk their talk.

• **Optimism.** A sense of optimism is the third required component of character for leaders. The leaders I interviewed had a strong sense of optimism. No matter how daunting or improbable the task they were facing, they always seemed to give people that Pygmalion lift, the sense that they could do it. They were purveyors of hope—it's their favorite four-letter word. Leaders have an overall perception that their goals can be met. No matter how daunting the tasks, they approach them as if they can be solved.

Feelings of helplessness and futility only yield a ghetto mentality, while optimism yields healthy results. Research shows the significance of optimism on the recovery of people with cancer. It is the best predictor of college success, much better than SAT scores or grade point averages. The best coaches, parents, and therapists are those who instill others with a sense of hope. The late George Burns was a perfect example of this sense of optimism. On his 90th birthday, Burns said, "I can't die—I'm booked."

In these times, organizations need to be agile and adaptive learners, and they need to retain the best and brightest. Leaders who wish to be successful must become social architects. The leader's challenge is to shape a corporate culture that builds self-esteem, sustains trust, preserves the dignity of work, develops human bonds, fosters open communications, allows for dissent, and encourages growth and learning.

### Why Is Leadership So Important?

A couple of years ago, a journalist asked me, "Why is leadership so significant today?" I said, "It has always been significant, and it will have a long shelf-life. In fact, it will outlast all of us because there will always be a need for leadership."

Of course, for some reason, leadership always looks better in the past than it does in the present. In the present, leadership always looks problematical. There are always ethical dilemmas, tough issues, and paradoxes to work through. And people are always yearning for clarification and direction.

I've been studying leadership for a long time because I have a strong desire to influence the way people think and hopefully even the way they behave. I stopped being a university president because I was more interested in having influence through voice than having power through position.

Now, I'm also humbled. I realize that writing and lecturing on leadership doesn't necessarily make people good leaders. If I gave a lecture on morality, it would not make people moral. But I feel that there's a chance that an idea, a thought, or a concept might make people think a little differently—and maybe by thinking differently, they will change their own behavior.

For instance, I once helped Intel create a corporate college where they don't bring in any outsiders to teach. The teachers are all executives of the company. The corporate college enables Intel executives to walk their talk because when you teach something, you really have to internalize it and embody it.

A good coach does only two or three things. He or she gives people license to tell the truth, provide reflective back talk to their truth-telling, and remind them what's important. I try to give people a slant on issues that they wouldn't otherwise get themselves. The difference between coaching and managing is interesting, because when you go to a coach, you are typically not defensive. For example, if you go to a tennis coach, you simply say, "Look, my backhand stinks," or "I'd like to get a better second serve." You are paying the coach to help you improve your game.

I spoke recently with a board member about a certain CEO, and he said, "I had a stopwatch on my last meeting with him, and for every hour, he talks for fifty minutes, and I talk for ten. He doesn't listen."

When I work with leaders, I shadow them. I'm with them for one or two days, and I observe how they operate. If a Fortune 500 chairman calls me and asks: "How do I get people to be more open with me?" I observe him and ask: "Does he solicit information? Has he thought about how to generate and sustain trust? Is he open himself? Does he know how to create trusting relationships? To what extent does he screen off negative feedback, both verbally and non-verbally? How many people does he involve in significant policy decisions?"

After observing him, I might remind him to think about the

implications of his decision from the point of view of unions, suppliers, stockholders, and other stakeholders. Or I might tell the CEO to what extent subordinates feel able to register healthy dissent.

I personally admire Jack Welch of General Electric. Jack is a "can-do" American cowboy. He was very authoritarian, and of course he was called "Neutron Jack" wherever he went—the building remained, but the people were gone. But he's transformed himself and the GE culture. He changed because he realized that if he and GE were going to grow and if he was ever going to make GE an adaptive learning organization, he had better change his ways. He's become something of a participative manager. He's doing it in an extraordinary way. When he took over GE, there were 160 strategic business units, now there are 16. There were, on average, twenty-nine levels of the hierarchy; now there are nine going toward five. I think he's a hero.

I call it the Sadat syndrome. Sadat grew up in a culture which for years demonized the Israelis, and the Israelis demonized the Egyptians. It was a remarkable hostility. And yet despite his nature, his socialization, and the cultural differences that divided the two nations, Sadat was able to transcend his culture and try some innovative, risky peace initiatives. Gorbachev, too, had the same remarkable ability. He could see that the Soviet Union was a third-rate economic power and a first-rate military power and that something had to be done.

The good CEOs encourage dissent. The bad ones are blind and keep repeating the same mistakes. And when they get thrown out, they wonder why.

# 2 6

## COPs AND ACEs

*Command and control must give way to empowerment.*

In my book *On Becoming a Leader*, I write about the new generation of corporate leaders and how they must transition from the industrial age to the information age. While I do see promising signs, I dare say that only 10 percent of the organizations that I've observed seem to be moving in this direction.

Most of us grew up with bureaucratic organizations that were dominated by a command-and-control orientation. It was memorialized by the prose of German writer and sociologist Max Weber, who was the first to bring to the world's attention that this bureaucratic machine model is a genius of the social invention to harness the manpower and the resources of the 19th century. Most organizations still have that kind of command-and-control, macho mentality.

If there are three words that would best describe the mind-set of that paradigm, they would be "control, order, and predict." It has an interesting acronym—COP. Bureaucracies are characterized by strong divisions of labor, specialization, hierarchies, and lots of levels.

The organizations of the future will resemble networks or modules. The successful ones will have flattened hierarchies and more cross-functional linkages. I would use three words to describe the new mind-set: "acknowledge, create, and empower." That also is an interesting acronym—ACE. I'm indebted

to management consultant Jim Selman and Roger Evered, a professor at the Naval Post Graduate School in Monterey, California,
for introducing me to the concept of COPs and ACEs.

Given the speed and complexity of change in our society,
affecting all management environments, I don't think we have
any alternative but to move away from COP toward ACE.

Leading based on ACE will require different leadership qualities. I was talking recently with the change maven of all times,
Alvin Toffler, whose book, *Future Shock*, came out in 1970. We
were trying to imagine, if we could, an organization that
presently exists that has been stable for 100 to 200 years and is
also prosperous. We couldn't think of one. So, if we were in a
stable, predictable environment where the established rules of
five years ago would work today, I would say, "Terrific, let's just
continue with the command-and-control, macho mind-set."

Maybe we've got to move from macho to maestro in the way
we're thinking about leading our organizations. Maestro is an
interesting metaphor because an orchestra, a symphony orchestra, is not a bad metaphor to think about with contemporary
organizations. They are filled with specialists, but have a flattened hierarchy.

### Caught in Dilemmas

The question I most often get when I talk to executive groups
is, "How do we change in a very successful organization those
behaviors of individuals who have been successful in the past,
but if they continue doing the things they've been doing in the
past, will not be successful in the future?" They have to unlearn
such things as talking rather than listening. They have to learn
such things as not just talking to people they're familiar with,
at home with, but individuals who may be different from them
in gender, in race, in ethnicity. How do we unlearn listening to
only a few people rather than a diverse group? All of these
things have to be unlearned in a new organizational structure.
So, it's not just what do people have to learn, it's how they're
going to unlearn those things that really brought them success
in the past. That's the tough issue.

Managers also ask me, "How do I create an empowered organization that encourages risk taking and still gets the bottom-
line results?" People working in middle management and lower

senior management positions are really caught in this dilemma. How do we create an empowered organization and at the same time still keep the numbers up? How do we keep our eye on the bottom line as well as on the horizon? How do we keep trying to do different things, but still stick to our knitting? How do we create an organizational culture that is a neat and marvelous place to work, have job security, and still get lean and mean, then get restructured? How do we do all those things and still raise terrific kids?

In effect, we're in between these two paradigms of control, order, and predict (COP) and acknowledge, create and empower (ACE). Effective leadership is what's needed to transcend all of that.

There is no substitute for top leadership. You have to be deeply involved, not simply sending down edicts and vision statements, but in fact translating the idea of empowerment into organizational realities. In other words, the only way the vision of empowerment can work is to sustain it through actions—actions of organization, actions of rewards, actions of recruiting, actions of communicating meaning, what it's all about. So the rhetoric unsustained through actions is simply going to be empty and create cynicism.

Another dilemma is that people are supposed to be zealously committed to visions and missions, yet remain agile, flexible, and adaptable. So the new game of change creates all sorts of tough dilemmas for management and leadership to take into account.

### Where Do We Go Wrong?

Whenever I ask managers or leaders what they attribute most of their mistakes to, they say it was when they didn't follow their instincts, their gut reactions—when they didn't trust their intuition. Lots of people have trouble getting to bedrock, of hearing signals and acting on them. I think that takes trying to understand everything from your body to those vagrant thoughts that may come into your mind.

How do you develop self-knowledge? I see some very simple things, such as getting feedback from valued sources or what I call reflective back talk, surrounding yourself with people honest enough to confront you and to provide valuable feedback. The reason I know this is because so many of the leaders I interviewed in my own work told me how significant their spouses are because they know they can rely on them for reflective back talk. So, find as many sources of valued feedback as you can because feedback is truly the "breakfast of champions."

Leaders also learn a lot from failure. Failure screams out for explanation. When I ask executives how they learn, they often tell me, "It's through mistakes, through mishaps, through falling on my butt—and not just once." But they also imply something else. Number one, that you are able to actually reflect upon those experiences. Number two, that you can see your own role. It's not only being able to reflect on an experience, it's being able to see what you've contributed to it.

All of the successful executives I interviewed had what I consider to be a slight distortion of their self-concept toward extreme optimism. So they kept on trying. They had a lot of "at bats." It wasn't just that they were good at explaining mistakes and failures. But, as one of them put it, "rejection is simply deferred success." They kept trying. I think that may be the key—the capacity to reflect on experience and to keep trying.

### On the Leading Edge of Change

Inevitably, global change has corporate repercussions. If there is reason to despair and join the doomsayers in handwringing and headshaking, it is because traditional American managers were brought up in a simple time, when all they had to do was build the best mousetraps and the world beat a path to their doors.

"Leadership in a traditional U.S. company," says R.B. Horton, CEO of British Petroleum America, "consisted of creating a management able to cope with competitors who all played with basically the same deck of economic cards." And it was an American game. The competition may have been fierce, but it was knowable. If you played your cards right, you could win.

But that game has changed dramatically, and strange new rules have appeared. The deck has been shuffled and jokers added. Never before has American business faced so many challenges. Uncertainties and complexities abound. There are too many ironies, polarities, confusions, contradictions, and ambivalences for any organization to understand fully. The only truly predictable thing right now is unpredictability.

In his book *Adhocracy: The Power to Change,* Bob Waterman tells us that most of us are like the characters in Ibsen's play *Ghosts:*

> *We're controlled by ideas and norms that have outlived their usefulness, that are only ghosts but have as much influence on our behavior as they would if they were alive. The ideas of men like Henry Ford, Frederick Taylor, and Max Weber—these are the ghosts that haunt our halls of management.*

### Recurring Themes

Over the past dozen years, interacting with and interviewing CEOs and leaders of all kinds, I have seen several themes appear again and again.

However much the CEOs differ in experience and personal style, they constitute a prism through which the fortunes of the modern world are refracted. These leaders are emblematic of their time, forced to deal not only with the exigencies of their own organizations but also with a new social reality. Among the broader factors that underlie all their decisions: the accelerating rate and complexity of change, the emergence of new technologies, dramatic demographic shifts, and globalization.

• Each of these leaders has discovered that the very culture of his or her organization must change because, as constituted, that culture is more devoted to perceiving itself than to meeting new challenges.

• Each of these individuals is a leader, not a manager.

• Each of these individuals understands that management is getting people to do what needs to be done. Leadership is getting people to want to do what needs to be done. Managers push. Leaders pull. Managers command. Leaders communicate.

• Without exception every CEO interviewed has become the Chief Transformation Officer of his or her organization.

John Sculley, former CEO of Apple, once told me:

> *The old hierarchical model is no longer appropriate. The new model is global in scale, an interdependent network. So the new leader faces new tests, such as how does he lead people who don't report to him—people in other companies, in Japan or Europe, even competitors.*

*How do you lead in this idea-intensive, interdependent network environment? It requires a wholly different set of skills, based on ideas, people skills, and values. Traditional leaders are having a hard time explaining what's going on in the world, because they're basing their explanations on their experience with the old paradigm.*

The organizations of the future will be networks, clusters, cross-functional teams, temporary systems, ad hoc task forces, lattices, modules, matrices—almost anything but pyramids. We don't even know yet what to call these new configurations, but we do know that the ones that succeed will be less hierarchical and have more linkages based on common goals rather than traditional reporting relationships. It is also likely that these successful organizations will embody Rosabeth Moss Kanter's "5 F's: fast, focused, flexible, friendly, and fun."

The CEOs I know best understand that contemporary organizations face increasing and unfamiliar sources of competition as a result of the globalization of markets, capital, labor, and information technology. To be successful, these organizations must have flexible structures that enable them to be highly responsive to customer requirements and adaptive to changes in the competitive environment. These new organizations must be leaner, have fewer layers, and be able to engage in transnational and nontraditional alliances and mergers. And they must understand a global array of business practices, customs, and cultures.

The question all these leaders are addressing, with apparent success, is: How do you change relatively successful organizations, which, if they continue to act today the way they acted even five years ago, will undo themselves in the future? (Remember that 47 percent of the companies that made up the Fortune 500 in 1980 were not on the list in 1990.)

### The ACE Paradigm

The CEOs are telling us that the new paradigm for success has three elements: Align, Create, and Empower, or ACE.

• **Align.** Today's leader needs to align resources, particularly human resources, creating a sense of shared objectives worthy of people's support and even dedication. Alignment has much to do with the spirit and a sense of being part of a team. Great organizations inevitably develop around a shared vision. Theodore Vail had a vision of universal telephone service that would take fifty years to bring about.  Henry Ford envisioned common people, not just the wealthy, owning their own automobiles. Steven Jobs, Steven Wozniak, and their Apple cofounders saw the potential of the computer to empower people. A shared vision uplifts people's aspirations. Work becomes part of pursuing a larger purpose embodied in products and services.

• **Create.** Today's leader must create a culture where ideas come through unhampered by people who are fearful. Such leaders are committed to problem-finding, not just problem-solving. They embrace error, even failure, because they know it will teach them more than success. As Norman Lear once said to me, "Wherever I trip is where the treasure lies."

Effective leaders create adaptive, creative, learning organizations. Such organizations have the ability to identify problems, however troublesome, before they become crises. These organizations are able to rally the ideas and information necessary to solve their problems. They are not afraid to test possible solutions, perhaps by means of a pilot program. And, finally, learning organizations provide opportunities to reflect on and evaluate past actions and decisions.

• **Empower.** Empowerment involves the sense people have that they are at the center of things, rather than the periphery. In an effectively led organization, everyone feels he or she contributes to its success. Empowered individuals believe what they do has significance and meaning. Empowered people have both discretion and obligations. They live in a culture of respect where they can actually do things without getting permission first from some parent figure. Empowered organizations are characterized by trust and system-wide communication.

Whatever shape the future ultimately takes, the organizations that will succeed are those that take seriously—and sustain through action—the belief that their competitive advantage is based on the development and growth of the people in them. And the men and women who guide those organizations will be a different kind of leader than we've been used to. They will be maestros, not masters, coaches, not commanders.

Today the laurel will go to the leader who encourages healthy dissent and values those followers brave enough to say no. The successful leader will have not the loudest voice, but the readiest ear. His or her real genius may well lie not in personal achievements, but in unleashing other people's talent.

# 27

## SHAKES AND QUAKES

*The big quake that rocked Southern California in January 1994 is symptomatic of the tremors shaking all of corporate America.*

The present world scene is so paradoxical, confusing, and filled with contradictions, dilemmas and ambiguities, that it's making life very difficult for everyone running a business. As organizations grow larger and as the changes become more turbulent and dramatic, the dual forces of size and change intersect to create inertia and arrogance.

CEOs are being dumped in unprecedented numbers. One reason is CEO ineptitude and arrogance, but another is simply that most organizations have a tough time finding the right people to lead in an environment of constant change.

Every organization I know is undergoing incredible, turbulent, profound change. The changes taking place right now in this country are so pervasive and so ubiquitous that my feeling is that they're more monumental and catastrophic than the changes in Eastern Europe.

To deal with all this change, executives have to have what I call the Wayne Gretzky factor. What's important, he says, is not where the hockey puck is but where it's going to be. That's what the responsibility of leaders is—vision and anticipation. It's not companies that fail; it's really their leaders who fail.

Sure, some conditions, quakes, storms, and events can't be forecast, but that doesn't let corporate leaders off the hook entirely. I don't think it would have been possible to foresee the collapse of Eastern European communism or the end of the Soviet Empire or the Yugoslav situation. But the fierce galloping toward globalization and advanced technology should not have been so difficult to foresee.

The basic questions for most organizations are: How do you lead change? How do you stay ahead of the curve in this era of enormous change? When I interviewed Colin Powell, the former Chairman of the Joint Chiefs of Staff, about his experiences as a leader, he pointed out that the first years of his career were easy in comparison to the last five years. Before, he always knew who the enemy was, their strengths and their tactics. Then General Powell participated with Presidents Reagan and Bush in meetings with Gorbachev. In about the fifth meeting, Gorbachev said he was going to change Russia so much that they would deny us our enemy. Once it happened, both the political and economic world changed.

Democratization, capitalism, the growth of technology, and the problems of oversupply are major change forces on their own. Combined, they have created an environment of seismic change. Finding people who can lead in such an environment is very challenging. Basically, you need people who can walk their companies into the future rather than back them into the future.

### Learning Environments

The key to gaining a competitive advantage will be the ability of leaders to create an adaptive learning environment that encourages the development of intellectual capital. Leaders like Jack Welch at General Electric, Roberto Goizueta at Coca-Cola, and Percy Barnevik at ABB have learned how to use their leadership to create environments that release the creative powers of individuals. Many CEOs who were pushed out of office didn't have that ability, an ability that will be even more crucial as we move into the next century.

Leaders are always made, not born. There is no genetic marker for leadership. Basically, leadership is learned on the job. In our studies at USC, we ask leaders how they learned to be leaders. They point to major challenges they faced and overcame—learning through mistakes and going forward. None say they learned leadership by taking academic courses or by getting an MBA or Ph.D. They learned the most from their bosses—both good and bad ones.

Why don't organizations do a better job of creating leaders? Part of the answer is that leaders challenge the system; they question the gospel. Most organizations, in times of change, don't reward that questioning behavior; they reward management that follows.

George Bernard Shaw said: "All great progress is made by unreasonable men who make the world adapt to them; and reasonable men adapt to the world."

Successful leaders recognize that we're moving to a stage of idea-intensive production and away from material-intensive production. They realize that if a leader's going to be successful, it's going to be through intellectual capital that creates wealth; that it's people with ideas who are making a difference.

I think it's a belief in magic that makes for greatness. Remember Walt Disney's famous dictum: "If you can dream it, you can do it." Part of leadership is magic. Remember the Grand Inquisitor section in *The Brothers Karamazov*? The Grand Inquisitor was angry at Christ, saying he's just involved with miracles and mystery. Well, frankly I think we need miracles and mystery.

But I don't want to make too much of magic. Basically, what leaders offer is intellectual capital, ideas, know-how. The key to competitive advantage is the capacity of top leadership to create a learning environment—an adaptive, agile, athletic, social architecture capable of generating intellectual capital.

All the great leaders I know ultimately are concerned with only three things: people, dollars, and ideas. If they pick the right people and allocate the right number of dollars to particular divisions, and if they break down the smokestack bureaucratic roles so the best practices get transferred immediately from one division to the next, then we're going to see successful corporations.

Large companies will have to try harder because they have these thick walls between divisions that make passing information and ideas back and forth much more difficult. The most successful corporations will not be content to go with status quo. General Electric was able to change without being forced;

it was able to reorganize and revitalize itself.

Few organizations are asking themselves: How do we build our leaders for the future? One thing we do know about leadership is that the larger the variety of horizontal assignments a person takes on in the organization, the more leadership talent the person develops. ARCO and Glaxo are examples of organizations that make sure their potential leaders get involved in every single aspect of their business throughout their careers.

Coaching will become the model for leaders in the future. Coaches teach, mentor, and empower. You have to be honest with them, and they with you. They help you focus on what's important now. All businesses need leaders to remind them every day what's important now at the same time they are defining a vision of the future.

### Ambition, Competence, Character

In my work with leaders, I emphasize the importance of character. Integrity is an essential ingredient of successful leaders. It's not only true of individuals, it is also true of great organizations.

I see a "tripod" of leadership: One leg is ambition or drive; another leg is competence or expertise; and the third leg is integrity or moral fabric. Imagine someone with just unbridled ambition, and you get a demagogue, a Stalin. Imagine someone with just competence, and you get a technocrat, someone who eventually destroys the soul of the organization.

In times of turbulence and change, people often pick a leader who has ambition and competence, but little integrity. Ultimately, those leaders fail—and the price their followers pay is enormous. If history tells us anything about leaders it's this: in picking a leader, insist on integrity.

So many leaders have put themselves in the position where they have to regain the trust of their employees. And with all the restructuring going on today, how do leaders regain trust? Changes, particularly those that mean a reduction in jobs, are never going to be popular. However, leaders don't have to pay for change with trust if their communication about change is honest, open, candid, and caring.

When I listen to leaders talk about changes and the impact on jobs, they all say that they can no longer promise job security, only "employability." If leaders provide people with the training needed to do the work and communicate well, they won't lose the trust of employees.

Another approach is to involve the employees in the restructuring so jobs can be saved. Rather than lay off workers, Sidney Harman, president of Harman Industries, is involving them in developing new uses for their products and in developing new products. For example, they now use some throwaway materials for making clock faces. They've turned other materials into trivets. They're also reclaiming some of the services they've been outsourcing—bringing those functions back inside, and making use of that surplus of space and people. That's creative, caring leadership.

A new kind of leader has emerged who is a facilitator, not an autocrat. An appreciator of ideas, not a fount of them. These leaders realize that they're basically coaches. As Max DePree once said, "You've got to abandon your ego to the talents of others."

I think that all good leaders have moved away from being macho to being a maestro, a conductor bringing out the best of each member of the orchestra.

Effective leaders are constant learners, inventing themselves as they go along. They hunger for knowledge. They learn from every position they are in. And they grow both in knowledge and in character. Look at Jack Welch, CEO of General Electric. "Look," he once said to me, "I had to be hard-nosed when I took over GE in 1981. We had 425,000 workers, and our revenue was about $25 billion. Today, our revenue is $65 billion, and we have 275,000 workers. Today, we have the companies we want and the people we want. Now I can be the coach and facilitator." He learned along the way and became a very effective leader.

Welch realizes that if he wants to keep the best and the brightest, if he wants a company that has its foundation in ideas, innovation, and learning, he's got to be the coach—the person who gets people to play at their best, who brings out the best of their ideas. That's what it's all about—ideas. Look at the so-called four Little Dragons: Taiwan, South Korea, Hong Kong, and Singapore. They have no resources. Technology can be copied overnight. What they have is the ability to utilize their people, using their brains. That's what it takes today.

How do leaders release the brainpower and creativity of people? How do they help create learning organizations? Many are evolving into confederations where decisions are made by the units that can best make them. The only reason for decisions to be made at the top is when something relates to everybody, or you need some synergy among units.

### Business Federations

In these turbulent times, any prudent map maker is working on an Etch-a-Sketch. Political boundaries are changing weekly, as new nations emerge with varying degrees of anguish from the disintegrating empires of yesterday.

No part of the world is exempt. From the Balkans to Northern Ireland, from the West Bank to Sri Lanka, in Africa, Asia and the Pacific Islands, tribes of people are wrestling, often at the cost of lives, with what I call the Iceland Dilemma.

After only a few hours in Iceland, it becomes clear that this bleakly beautiful country is being shaped by two powerful but opposing forces. On the one hand, its 250,000 citizens are fiercely proud of their Viking heritage. They are so proud that they have a committee to give Viking names to concepts even the most visionary Viking could not have imagined. Thus, in Iceland a computer screen is called a skjar, named for another kind of window, that on a traditional turf house.

But that passion for what is uniquely theirs is only one side of modern Iceland. Even as Icelanders quote the sagas and support laws that require citizens to bear only approved Icelandic names, those same citizens are eager to enter into an exogamous marriage with the European community, joining their fortunes to those of people who have little or no interest in the purity of Icelandic tongue.

Iceland is a particularly vivid example of what philosophers used to call the tension between the tribal and the universal. How to balance tradition and the desire for change, how to actualize oneself while being a partner, how to sing solo and in chorus at the same time? That is the Iceland Dilemma—the need to strike a balance between nationalism and globalism— and it is one the whole world is grappling with.

In many nations and organizations, we witness the tension between localism and transnationalism. We see it in Russia, in

Yugoslavia, in Quebec, even in California. By the end of this
century we are going to see some very different configurations
of states and nations. We're living in a world with over 5,000
nationalities and only 190 nation-states. Nobody knows quite
what to do. That's why we need to think of new forms. I am
convinced there is a solution to the Iceland Dilemma. It's the
one that has been tried before with notable success in countries
as different as Canada and Spain. That solution is federation.

Unlike monolithic governments, federations are alliances of
more or less independent states, often with little in common
but their desire to share in the benefits of unity. Perhaps the
most durable argument for federation is Switzerland, where a
workable union of divergent cultures has survived for more than
700 years. Today there are twenty-six autonomous cantons and
half-cantons in Switzerland, representing four major cultural
groups, each with its own language and customs. That alliance
endures despite a remarkable diversity of values, including
those of one reactionary half-canton that has yet to give women
the vote in local elections!

Federation allows member states to realize their distinctive
possibilities and address their distinctive needs, as long as they
don't compromise the rights of other members or the needs of
the alliance. In successful federations, which must include our
own resilient alliance, the whole is greater than the sum of
Alabama, Alaska, Arizona and all its other disparate, but essential, parts.

Federations work, especially in rapidly changing times such
as ours, because they offer flexibility as well as strength. By
their very nature, federations acknowledge the existence of
alternatives, of more than one possible response to a given challenge. If federation were a poem, it would be, not the epic saga
of a national hero, but something like Wallace Steven's
"Thirteen Ways of Looking at a Blackbird."

Committed to a single vision, the national monolith is often
too slow to respond to new realities. Federations are nimble by
nature, trained in a repertoire of responses, not limited to a single national stance. Monoliths go for all or nothing. Federations
multiply the options and reduce the risk. Federations are also
far less prone to the racism and ethnic hatred that is one of the
ugliest aspects of hyper-patriotism. Federations implicitly

acknowledge that diversity is strength. In homogeneous groups, the other is too easily seen as a monster, a devil, and an obstacle on the road to racial or ethnic purity. It is much harder to vilify and dehumanize the other in heterogenous alliance in which the other, however different, is viewed as a peer, even a partner.

Not surprisingly, federation is a major trend in business as well as politics. Many of the world's most influential business leaders are creating a new kind of corporate confederation, one in which semi-autonomous units, often in far-flung countries, join together to succeed in an increasingly global economy. The best example is probably Percy Barnevik, whose worldwide federation of companies, Asea Brown and Boveri, has become a model for global orchestration of component units skilled at exploiting the specific realities of their home countries. Jack Welch, chairman and CEO of General Electric, also uses the rhetoric of the new corporate confederation when he talks about a "borderless" organization.

I can imagine a time when corporations such as ABB, that are simultaneously global and deeply rooted in local cultures, will serve as models for nations that aspire both to national self-expression and to survival in the world economy. These new federations could solve the Iceland Dilemma once and for all. And I suspect the only cost will be the loss of the sort of jingoistic rhetoric that state mottoes and national anthems have traditionally been made of. The slogans of the federations of the future probably won't be as stirring as the national slogans of the past. "My federation, a pretty good alliance" doesn't have the ring of "My country, right or wrong," it's true. But it could be a far better place to work and live.

How do you empower organizations when you are restructuring? How do you empower both the survivors and those who have left? This is where we need some government and business partnering—a policy of re-education to handle the period of dislocation and transition. But re-education isn't enough. Companies, before they restructure, have to utilize the brainpower of the people there.

The basic job of leadership is to create an organizational form that will release the brainpower of people. I don't know what that form looks like, but we're not entirely clueless. There are many evolving organizational structures, including temporary systems, cluster organizations, loosely coupled organizations, networks, teams, and many others. But it clearly isn't going to be a pyramidal bureaucracy with the mind-set of control, order, and predict. It's going to be a variety of different forms which align, create, and empower—and these forms will probably be changing all the time.

# 28

## DEALING WITH THE
## WAY THINGS ARE

*After we identitfy the real problems and the true villains,
we then need to see and do things in new ways.*

Alfred North Whitehead cautioned us to "seek simplicity
and then distrust it." Unfortunately, too many people seek
and accept simplistic solutions for complex problems and
never question them at all. As a result, the latest miracle drug
has dangerous side effects, lawmakers enact bills and then discover consequences that they never imagined, manufacturers
develop great new products that are more trouble than they
are worth, and CEOs bring in expensive consultants who create chaos rather than order.

We are so intent now on finding answers that we listen
earnestly to anyone who claims to be an expert. The fact is
that there are too many predicaments, grievances, ironies,
polarities, dichotomies, dualities, ambivalences, paradoxes,
contradictions, confusions, complexities, and messes, and so
we naturally incline toward people with answers—without
even bothering to wonder what the real questions are. But
until we begin asking the right questions, we cannot possibly
come up with the right answers. Rather than trying to figure
out the questions, however, we accept any answer, no matter
how spurious, or find a convenient villain.

The airlines said that regulations were hampering them.
Today, deregulation is killing them. The auto industry said
that government fiats were murdering it. Today, it begs the

government to kill the foreign competition. When the White House goofs, it blames the media.

Instead of seeking easy answers and scapegoats, it's time for us to grow up and start using our heads to identify the real problems and the true villains. Simplistic solutions are usually the forerunners of people who thrive on them—such as political bosses and TV ministers. Our collective incapacity to tolerate ambiguity in the face of enormously complicated problems has led us to an almost automatic acceptance of instant relief. Some of us turn to drugs, others to exotic rituals and gurus, others to very conspicuous consumption, and all of us, at one time or another, to "experts."

Sooner or later, we must accept the fact that complexity is here to stay, and that order begins in chaos. William Blake wrote, "Without contraries, there is no progression." The instant solution almost always expunges significant options.

### Seeing Things in New Ways

Until dull parents, teachers, or peers turn them into automatons, children have the instinctive ability to see things in new or different ways, and so do leaders. In fact, there are many resemblances between poets, children, and leaders. All are simple, but never simplistic; all are full of questions and skeptical of easy answers; all trust their instincts, and all are capable of simultaneous truth and originality.

Consider any true American leader, from Thomas Jefferson to Henry Ford to Martin Luther King. Each was a dreamer yet practical, an original yet totally in sync with his constituents, and each made something new. Jefferson made our Declaration of Independence, Ford gave us a vehicle that made us independent, and King gave us a dream that might have made us all free, if we had had the courage to make the dream real.

But the great leaders are gone and, with them, our dreams. Everything is subject to change now. Peter Drucker has said:

> *We are witnessing what may be the death of the large company. The flagships of the last forty years, institutions like General Motors, ITT and Du Pont, have basically outlived their usefulness. I think they're past their peaks. There's very little flexibility there, very lit-*

*tle creativity. There are a lot of tasks for which you need bigness, yes, but in a society with institutions of only one size—and it's a large size—in a time of transition and change, you lack something vital: the ability to experiment, the ability to fail without disastrous consequences. There are no greater failures than our present business school graduates, outside of the narrowest financial sphere. The Harvard Business School graduates are abysmal failures, because the Business School assumes, for example, an elite, homogenous America, and we're the most diversified country in the world.*

Traditional structures are changing, the current greediness will subside, but we the people stand pat. In such circumstances, people in positions of authority are, at best, agents of adjustment, striving to face things as they are and prepare for things as they will be. America is in all kinds of trouble—from Wall Street to Main Street.

Why? Perhaps because we've lost the ability to work together—even for profit. Teamwork is, after all, antithetical to our current mode, but our inability to work together, to collaborate and cooperate, is undermining America.

### Ten Things to Be or Do

People in positions of authority who hope to make a difference in the way things are might try the following:

• **Be alert, curious, impatient, brave, steadfast, truthful, and in focus;** you must not only know what you see but say what you see. Gandhi said, "We must be the change we wish to see in the world." Thus, if you believe that competence and conscience must be restored, then you must demonstrate both.

There are no easy answers, no quick fixes, no formulas. It's time to face facts, lest we all follow Boesky, North, Hart, and the Bakkers into the abyss. We are not supermen. We cannot remake the world to suit us. It's not some mere trick of fate that the high and the mighty are tumbling off their pedestals; rather it is the inevitable result of ambition outstripping competence and conscience. Whatever the question, competence and conscience are part of the answer, and unless we accept that fundamental fact, we will all, sooner or later, fall down.

• **Develop the vision and authority to call the shots.** There are always risks in taking the initiative, but there are greater risks now in waiting for sure things, especially since there are very few sure things in the current volatile climate. At the same time, the people have to admit their need for leadership, for vision, for dreams.

• **Do more than tinker with the machinery and flex your muscles.** You must have an entrepreneurial vision, a sense of perspective, along with the time and inclination to raise the fundamental questions and identify the forces that are at work on both specific organizations and society in general. Such tasks require not only imagination but a real sense of continuity so that, to paraphrase Shelley, one can see the present in the past and the future in the present, clarify problems rather than exploit them, and define issues, not exacerbate them. In this way, you can elevate problems, questions, and issues into comprehensible choices.

• **Be educators.** Our great political leaders have always tried to educate the people by transforming their messy existential groaning into understandable issues. The chieftain who responds to a drought by attacking the lack of rainfall will inspire no confidence at all. Instead of merely labeling problems—for example, "the economy"—you must analyze them and offer clear alternatives.

• **Be social architects,** shaping "the culture of work," examining the values and norms and the ways these are transmitted to individuals, and, where necessary, altering them. Whatever your goals, you must create means that will facilitate understanding and encourage participation, making sure your goals are in synch with the needs and aspirations of your followers. Trust, especially today, does not come easily: it must be earned. CEOs who believe that trust comes automatically, along with the perks, salary, and power, are in for some rude surprises. You must permit yourself to be influenced by the people you presume to lead; otherwise, your plans, however fine, will be subverted.

An organization's culture dictates the mechanisms needed to resolve conflicts and determines how costly, humane, fair, and reasonable the outcomes will be. New CEOs, then, must devote themselves to understanding the culture and altering it to suit their goals. The smart CEO also banishes the sort of zero-sum mentality that insists on absolute winners and absolute losers in favor of a climate of hope and reconciliation.

Any culture emerges out of its particular history, geography, technology and philosophy. No two are alike. Some are relaxed and coherent; others are frenzied and chronically cranky. One can "read" an organization's culture by talking with any employee as well as measuring the character and posture of its top person. Each employee is, to a remarkable extent, the organization in miniature. A chief executive must be something of a social anthropologist and architect, to maintain or change the culture.

• **Know yourself and listen to yourself,** integrating your ideals and actions while tolerating the gap between the desirable and the necessary as you work to close it. Know how to not merely listen but hear, not merely look but see, to play as hard as you work, and to live with ambiguity and inconsistency. The ultimate test is to successfully ride and direct the tides of change and, in doing so, grow stronger. As Sophocles said in *Antigone*, "It is hard to learn the mind of any mortal, or the heart, till he be tried in chief authority. Power shows the man." And the thoughtful, imaginative, and effective use of power is what separates leaders from people in authority.

Leadership is more practice than theory, and it is practiced in the real world, not a laboratory. The leader's world is divided into two camps: people who answer to him or her, and people he or she answers to. Leaders' decisions are inevitably influenced by both camps. The people they are responsible for now demand more from them—on both traditional questions such as conditions in the workplace, and new questions, such as maternity leaves. The people they are responsible to—from boards and shareholders to local, state, and federal governments to customers or constituents—have never been more vocal and more trigger-happy.

Then, of course, there are the omnipresent, omnivorous media, who are frequently used by adversaries and who are themselves sometimes adversaries. This not only traps leaders in a kind of constant spotlight but requires them to do much of their work in public. Business-oriented media have limited focus but apparently unlimited license to cover the field, and so leaders are required to play to the media while avoiding playing for them.

• **Design the actual structure of succession** in addition to setting goals and policies to achieve those goals, inspiring followers to work toward those goals, and creating an encouraging and functional climate. In too many cases, middle management is crippled by isolation. As people proceed up the ladder, they are enclosed by norms, beliefs, and values that are peculiar to middle management. When they finally get to the top, a whole new array of forces—environmental, political, economic and financial—confronts them in forms they have never had to consider. Nothing in their prior experience prepares them for the job they have been aiming at from the moment they joined the organization.

• **Create a transitive organization,** so that job A prepares one for job B, which, in turn, prepares one for job C. In the bookkeeping-finance trajectory, the career line is intransitive. This linear but illogical sort of structure is the real basis for the Peter Principle: People inevitably rise to the level of their own incompetence. At the same time, the leader should incorporate a reflective arena into his or her structure, so that time out for musing is mandatory. I'm not suggesting the sort of retreats that organizations have recently become so fond of, because they are usually the same old routine in a new locale. If executives stopped regularly to think about what they were doing, they would have the fresh insights they now pay consultants dearly for. As perspective is vital to the painter or writer, it is vital to leaders and their associates.

• **Create a means for managing conflict.** Both the culture of work and the structure of the organization must also contain intangibles, such as opportunities for everyone at every level to learn in order to maintain and improve job satisfaction, a stated code of ethics to establish and maintain honesty and probity, and the means to manage and resolve differences and conflicts.

Conflict is inevitable, and it can be destructive or useful, depending on how the leader handles it. Leaders create environments in which opportunity, honesty, and a kind of automatic mediation device exist. Leaders do not avoid, repress, or deny conflict, but rather see it as an opportunity. Once everyone has come to see it that way, they can exchange their combative posture for a creative stance, because they don't feel threatened, they feel challenged.

• **Express the unspoken dreams of people.** The leader knows what we want and what we need before we do and expresses these unspoken dreams for us in everything he or she says and does. When Martin Luther King spoke of his dream, for a moment, all of us, black and white alike, were one. Of course, now we are all wiser, and more cynical, and we don't believe in dreams anymore. But deep in all of us there is still and always will be a need to believe, and one day a leader will appear who will express that need, and fulfill it.

These are hard times for leaders. This era is characterized by material growth, humanity over nature, competitive self-interest, rugged individualism, a belief that large is beautiful, specialized work roles, standardized products, and a generally stressful existence. We are defined by our patterns of consumption and work status, not by who we are but by what we do.

Once we believed that success was achieved through hard work, frugality, industry, diligence, prudence, and honesty. Now we believe that success is based on our personality alone. If we can please other people, we will succeed. Instead of working at work, we work on our personalities. Instead of being good at what we do, we opt for charm. And we do not dream, we fantasize.

The country itself seems stalled in some kind of limbo, going neither to the left nor the right. We are not becoming reactionary or radical. When we respond to problems at all, we respond ambidextrously: right, left, right, left. Perhaps a certain ambivalence is appropriate; remaining open to redefinitions is necessary, and admitting of a future that is unlike the past is essential. After all, as the guru of the Beat Generation, Jack Kerouac, said, "Walking on water wasn't built in a day."

But true leaders are not deterred by hard times. That is perhaps, finally, what makes them leaders. As Abigail Adams wrote long ago to Thomas Jefferson, "Great necessities call forth great leaders."

# 29

## WINNING AND LOSING

*Thinking of business in sports terms is risky; a company competes more with itself than with its competition.*

Americans are, on the whole, simple and direct people. Unlike Europeans, we do not incline toward nuances or subtleties, in either our lives or our work. Unlike Asians, we opt inevitably for the concrete over the abstract. For these reasons, sports are not only our favorite form of entertainment, but our principal paradigm.

We talk often of winning and losing, scoring touchdowns, close calls, going down to the wire, extra innings, and while we may like movie, television and music stars, we admire sports stars. Every father wants his sons to shine on the playing fields, which is why Little League games frequently have all the carefree airs of the London blitz.

Preachers and politicians, among others, see this national obsession as healthy, portraying us as good, clean people interested in good, clean fun. Universities, including the University of Southern California where I teach, celebrate and reward their hero-athletes. On the day of the Super Bowl, the entire country's collective consciousness is focused on The Game.

### Time for a New Paradigm

I am admittedly as obsessed as anyone. I can remember great plays, great players, even scores of great games forever,

211

though I sometimes can't remember whom I sat next to at dinner three nights ago. But I am also convinced that it's time to find a new paradigm.

Life is not a baseball game. It's never called on account of darkness, much less cancelled due to inclement weather. And while major sports are big business now, business is not a sport, and never was. Indeed, thinking of business as a kind of game or sport was always simplistic. Now it's downright dangerous.

A game is of limited duration, takes place on or in a fixed and finite site, is governed by predetermined rules which are enforced on the spot by neutral professionals, and is performed by evenly matched teams of one or more who are counselled and led through every move by seasoned hands. Absolute scores are kept, and at the end of the game, an absolute winner is declared.

If there is anyone out there who can say that his or her business is of limited duration, takes place on a fixed site, is governed by rules which are enforced on the spot by neutral professionals, competes only with evenly matched businesses, and can describe its wins and losses in absolute terms, then he or she is either extraordinarily lucky or seriously deluded.

### The Risks

The risks in thinking of business in sports terms are numerous.

First, to measure a business on the basis of wins and losses is to misunderstand both the purposes of a specific business and the nature of business itself. No business—whether it sells insurance or manufactures cars—can or should be designed to win. It must rather be designed to grow, on both quantitative and qualitative levels. In this sense, it vies more with itself than with its competition. This is not to say that, in head-to-head contests, as when two ad agencies are competing for the same account, there are not ever winners and losers. It is to say, in paraphrase of Vince Lombardi's legendary dictum, winning isn't everything, it's one of many things a business must accomplish. Thus, a company that is designed only to deliver the knock-out punch will probably lose in the long run.

Second, it is perilous to think of limits, rules, and absolutes in business. Athletes compete for a given number of hours in a given number of games over a given period of weeks or months.

Businesses are in the arena for decades, sometimes centuries. Though the action may rise and subside, it never stops. It does not offer any time-outs, much less neatly defined beginnings and endings. As they say, it ain't over till it's over.

American business has traditionally been schizophrenic about rules. When it's flourishing, it wants no rules or regulations. When it's failing, it wants a plethora of rules. Some of the airlines which lobbied vigorously for deregulation have now, ironically, gone down in flames, victims of the very instrument they agitated for. In the same way, Detroit saw Washington as its nemesis, until foreign cars began to take over the market. Suddenly, Chrysler went to the feds for a loan, and now Detroit begs Washington to regulate the imports, but continues to lobby against federal safety and quality controls.

Athletes perform in a static environment—the size of the field, the length of the contest, even the wardrobes of the players remain the same day after month after year. Businesses function in a volatile universe, which changes from moment to moment, and is hardly ever repeated. It is affected by droughts half a world away, a new gizmo down the street, consumer attitudes and needs, a million things. Given this mercurial context, any business which relies on absolutes will soon be out of step or out of business.

Clearly, then, there are far more differences between sports and business than similarities. But the real danger in the paradigm is not its bad match, but its bad example.

The best-run and most successful companies in America do not think in terms of victories and defeats, shining moments or last-minute saves. They do not count on regulations or referees. Instead, they think in terms of staying power, dedication to quality, and an endless effort to do better than they have done. They see change as their only constant and count on their own ability to adapt to the world, rather than expecting the world to adapt to them. Indeed, it is a business's ability to adapt to an ever-changing world that is the basis for both its success and progress.

The truth is that there is no workable or appropriate paradigm for business, except business itself, and that should be sufficient. Like a well-played game, a well-run business is something to see, but, unlike a well-played game, it is not a diversion; it is life itself—complex, difficult, susceptible to both success and failure, sometimes unruly, always challenging, and often joyful.

So let's leave the home runs to Mike Schmidt and the touchdowns to Walter Payton, and get down to business.

# 30

## A NEW WAKE-UP CALL

*In today's more democratic organizations, new leaders are*
*needed to enhance the ability to adapt to change.*

The global challenges and changes of the emergent millennium—technological, cultural, environmental, and competitive—compel the creation of both new forms of organizations and new forms of leadership.

Existing public bureaucracies and private pyramidal organizations are as inadequate to a world of change, diversity, and interdependence as are existing models of leaders and followers. Traditional leadership metaphors—rulers and subjects, generals and foot soldiers, bosses and subordinates, coaches and players, fathers and families, shepherds and sheep—are inappropriate for an era of democracy and participation.

Peter Drucker's 1946 *Concept of the Corporation* was an unanswered wake-up call for American industry. He argued that there would be a radical transformation of the global business environment (he predicted revolutions in quality, technology, and service) and that corporations would have to undergo radical change to keep apace (he recommended paying attention to customers and ending adversarial labor relations). Most of corporate America slept through Drucker's call, and we are now witnessing the consequences of those decades of "extra winks."

Now is the time to set the alarm for the next millennium. To that end, my colleagues and I at USC invited a dozen or so individuals who possessed the most creative minds in the field of business management to participate in a symposium on "Reconceptualizing the Corporation: The Role of Leadership."

We asked some tough questions: 1) How is the world changing economically, socially, culturally, politically, technologically, environmentally, and competitively? 2) How must corporations change in order to meet the challenges of such transformations? and 3) What are the tasks and responsibilities of those who would lead organizations capable of making such changes?

Our aim was to develop leaders of leaders. In the fields of journalism, science, and the arts, there are places where leaders in their respective fields can engage in the 3Rs: Retreat, Reflect, and Refocus. Unfortunately, there is no such sabbatical place for executives—in particular, for those undergoing career transitions. We're serving as a laboratory for the creation of the New Leadership, hoping to prepare the next generation of leaders for a 21st century characterized by greater diversity, technological complexity, social and organizational democracy, and global interdependence.

Cynical observers have always pointed out that business leaders, who extol the virtues of democracy on ceremonial occasions, would be the last to think of applying them to their own organizations. To the extent that this is true, however, it reflects a state of mind that is by no means peculiar to business executives but characterizes all Americans, if not all citizens of democracies. This attitude is that democracy is a nice way of life for nice people, despite its manifold inconveniences—a kink of expensive and inefficient luxury, like owning a large medieval castle. Feelings about it are for the most part affectionate, even respectful, yet a little impatient. Few people in America have not at some time nourished in their hearts the blasphemous thought that life would go much more smoothly if democracy could be relegated to some kind of Sunday morning devotion.

The bluff partiality of the "nice but inefficient" stereotype masks a hidden idealism, however, for it implies that institutions can survive in a competitive environment through the sheer good-heartedness of those who maintain them. I challenge this notion. Even if all those benign sentiments were eradicated today, we would awaken tomorrow to find democracy still entrenched, buttressed by a set of economic, social, and political forces as practical as they are uncontrollable. Given a desire to survive and succeed, democracy is the most effective means to the end.

### Democracy Takes Over

Business and industry are finally becoming aware of democracy's efficiency. Several rapidly blooming companies boast unusually democratic organizations. Even more surprising, some large, established corporations have been moving steadily, if accidentally, toward democratization. Feeling that administrative vitality and creativity were lacking in their systems, the corporations enlisted the support of social scientists and consultants to democratize their organizations.

Executives, even entire management staffs, have participated in human relations and organizational development seminars to learn skills and attitudes that until recently would have been denounced as anarchic and revolutionary. At such meetings, status prerogatives and traditional concepts of authority are severely challenged.

My idea of "democracy" is not "permissiveness" or "laissez-faire" but a system of values—a climate of beliefs governing behavior—that people are internally compelled to affirm by deeds as well as words. These values include: full and free communication, regardless of rank and power; a reliance on consensus rather than on coercion or compromise to manage conflict; the idea that influence is based on technical competence and knowledge rather than on the vagaries of personal whims or prerogatives of power; an atmosphere that permits and even encourages emotional expression as well as task-oriented behavior; a bias that accepts the inevitability of conflict between the organization and the individual but mediates this conflict on rational grounds. Changes along these dimensions are being promoted widely today, because democracy becomes a functional necessity whenever a social system is competing for survival under conditions of chronic change.

### Adaptability to Change

If change has now become a permanent and accelerating factor in American life, then adaptability to change becomes the most important determinant of survival. The profit, the saving, the efficiency, and the morale of the moment become secondary to keeping the door open for rapid readjustment to changing conditions.

This change has come about because of the palpable inadequacy of the military-bureaucratic model, particularly its response to rapid change, and because science has emerged as a more suitable model. Science is winning out because the challenges facing modern enterprises are knowledge-gathering, truth-requiring dilemmas. Managers are not scientists, but the processes of problem solving, conflict resolution, and recognition of dilemmas have great kinship with the academic pursuit of truth. Science is the only institution geared for change—it is built not only to adapt to change but also to overthrow and create change.

For the spirit of inquiry to grow and flourish, there must be a democratic environment. Science encourages a political view that is egalitarian, pluralistic, liberal. It accentuates freedom of opinion and dissent. It is against all forms of totalitarianism, dogma, mechanization, and blind obedience. As a prominent social psychologist has pointed out, "Men have asked for freedom, justice, and respect precisely as science has spread among them." In short, the only way organizations can ensure a scientific attitude is to provide the democratic social conditions where one can flourish.

Democracy in business and industry is not an idealistic conception but a hard necessity in those areas where change is ever present and creativity must be nourished. Democracy is the only system of organization that is compatible with perpetual change. Corporations must be prepared to go anywhere—to develop new products or techniques even if they are irrelevant to present activities. The beginnings of democratization have appeared most often in industries that depend heavily on invention, such as electronics. This is undoubtedly why more and more sprawling behemoths are planning consequential changes in their structures and climates to release democratic potential.

In international politics, democratization is a recent phenomenon, although a profound one. The democratization of the workplace has made fewer headlines but has been no less dramatic. In the 1960s, participative management was a radical enough notion that some of the Sloan fellows at MIT accused me of being a Communist for espousing it. Now most major corporations practice some form of it. The pyramid-shaped organization chart has gone the way of the Edsel.

The change is pervasive. Self-managed work groups are replacing assembly lines in auto plants. Organizations as disparate as Herman Miller, the manufacturer of office furniture, and Beth Israel Hospital in Boston have adopted the democratic management techniques of the late Joseph Scanlon, one of the first to appreciate that employee involvement is crucial for quality control. At Hewlett-Packard's facility in Greeley, Colorado, most decisions are made not by traditional managers but by frontline employees who work in teams and contribute to parts of projects.

No longer a monolith, the new corporation is a Lego set whose parts can be readily reconfigured as circumstances change. The old paradigm that exalted control, order, and predictability has given way to a nonhierarchical order: contributions are solicited and acknowledged, and creativity is valued over blind loyalty. Sheer self-interest motivated the change. Organizations that encourage broad participation, even dissent, make better decisions and better forecasts.

Adaptability has become central to survival, as information now drives the new organization. The person who has information wields more power than ever before. New technology has accelerated the pace of change and helped create a global corporation, if not a global village. With computers and fax machines, New York Life Insurance processes its claims not in New York or even the United States but in Ireland. Several years ago, I invited the Dalai Lama to participate in a seminar for CEOs at the University of Southern California. The embodiment of thousands of years of Tibetan spiritualism graciously declined, by fax.

### New Organizations, New Leaders
So the new leader is a facilitator, not an autocrat, an appreciator of ideas, not necessarily a fount of them. The Great Man—or Woman—still exists as the public face of companies and countries, but the leader and the organization are no longer one and the same. The generals are being ousted and the poets

are taking charge—adopting a democratic model that not only tolerates change, but creates it. Democracy recognizes that creativity, an invaluable commodity, is utterly unpredictable and can come from any quarter.

The new leader strives for three elements, which, if realized, bring about effective, productive, creative change: empowerment, alignment, and an ability to adapt and learn. Adaptive, learning organizations work around a four-part learning wheel: 1) identification of troublesome problems; 2) the ideas and information to solve the problems; 3) the guts to test their solutions, at least on a pilot basis; and 4) opportunities to reflect and evaluate. The new leaders create a compelling vision, communicate the vision, sustain the vision. They also manage attention to bring others to a place they have never been before.

Some people get all tied up in knots. They keep adhering to earlier scripts, using the same lecture notes and repeating the same mistakes. Those people have forgotten how to learn. Basically, learning requires only two things: learning to be truthful, and learning to remember what's important. Good leaders give people the license to tell the truth and remind them what is important.

When people ask me how they can become better leaders, I tell them to start by asking themselves a few questions: "What is good in my life?" "What needs to be done?" "When do I feel most alive?" These questions help them to figure out what they really want. The people who are confused in this very ambiguous world are those people who have never figured out what they want.

### Authentic Leadership

I believe in self-invention. To be authentic is literally to be your own author, to discover your native energies and find your own way of acting upon them—not existing simply to live up to an image posited by the culture or some other authority.

Most effective business leaders reinvent themselves in important ways in response to the volatile, complex, turbulent, ambiguous, surprising, fluid changes in our society.

Given these changes, how can we not—if we want to continue to grow—keep from overhauling who we are? The world is different, and we've got to react differently to it—to realize, for example, that we don't have to be a brutal boss; we need to be an empowering, participative manager.

Einstein's definition of insanity is to repeat over and over the same practice, hoping to get different results. The problem with many companies is that they have been insane. When you're successful, it's hard to change. All companies are subject to insanity.

I feel for the people in the middle of an organization, because it's more difficult than if you're on the periphery. If you're a salesperson out in the field, the opportunities for learning are a lot better. The real initiatives come from the periphery—from creative people at the margins.

If you are going to succeed in business today you're going to have to develop people. Wealth is a function of ideas and know-how. It's important for people in any position to work in a situation where they can grow and develop.

I think you should talk with the boss directly, one-on-one. And if that doesn't work, go around and talk to other people and maybe even to the boss's boss. And if that doesn't work, you have to leave.

Is it cavalier or callous of me to recommend that? In the long run that business is going to fail if it doesn't change its ways, so the end result is the same.

It's like staying in a bad marriage because you're frightened by the prospect of being too old to remarry and not being in a financial position to strike out on your own again. So you stuff it all down and say, "I'm going to stay in a lousy relationship because the alternatives are worse." Often, the alternatives are better—if you act on them.

The best people have a bias toward action. They keep saying, "You're never going to get anywhere if you keep sitting in the dugout." The only way you're going to succeed, ultimately, in whatever you do, is to get up there and take your swings. And sometimes that means taking a swing at someone else who you think is doing something wrong or dangerous for the company. That's action, too.

Most of the 150 millionaires that I've interviewed said they've learned more from failure than from success. They possess the ability to learn from themselves and their mistakes, and what they do to get the best and worst out of people.

There is nothing like power to reveal your own humanity and character—especially power in crisis situations, because that's when you've hit rock bottom. As one CEO told me, "That's when the iron enters your soul, and gives you resiliency to cope." There's nothing like being a person of responsibility that teaches you about who you are. Nothing.

We've gone about 50 percent of the way in terms of intellectual acceptance of participative management and employee involvement. Where we still need to go further is in the capacity of tough leadership to create a social architecture that will generate intellectual capital—ideas, innovations, learning, know-how. That's what it's all about.

# REFLECTIONS ON RETIREMENT

*Retirement for anyone, but expecially for executives,*
*can mean adventure, risk, and great promise.*

The word "retirement" does not have a very positive connotation. Despite the upbeat books written about retiring and the fact that it is a well-earned time of relaxation from the daily business of work, many people do not find it a particularly pleasant prospect. The etymology of the word "retire" may hint at why. The ultimate source of the word is the old French word "retirer," made up of the prefix "re" meaning back and the verb "tirer" to draw together, meaning to withdraw, to take back. The first English use recorded in 1553 refers to a military force that withdraws and retreats. In regard to the sting in this, we need to look at the source of the word "tirer," meaning to draw out or to endure.

This word came from the old French "martir," in English "martyr" reflecting the fact that martyrs had to endure the torture of being stretched to and beyond the point of dislocating their bones. That's an interesting background for the word "retirement."

Aside from not being happy with the word "retirement," I'm not completely pleased with the euphemisms for retired people such as "senior citizens" or "seasoned citizens."

The second reason for my discomfort is that retirement is a topic that is relatively new to me and to my thinking. I've never discussed the issue. I've just begun to think about retirement and have tried to understand my resistance to the topic. I think

I had to work that through before I could even address this subject.

And, finally and most personally, having reached the age of seventy, I began thinking, maybe it's denial. (Is it the Grateful Dead who have a line in a song that goes, "Denial ain't just a river in Egypt"?) And I began thinking about that a little bit more. I guess I was jolted out of my denial when I was attending a conference in Monterey and somebody came up to me and said, "Didn't you used to be Warren Bennis?"

### Two Basic Ideas
I wish to share two basic ideas.

1. One idea was prompted by a question I was asked by a magazine on aging. During the course of the interview, the writer asked me who my heroes were and who I most respected for their response to the whole aging phenomenon. The people's names I rattled off were the following: Winston Churchill, Bertrand Russell, Clint Eastwood, Mel Torme, Colin Powell, Bill Bradley, Grace Hopper and Katherine Graham. I began thinking. What do they all have in common?

Well, Churchill really didn't get started on his career until he was 66. It was said about Churchill in one of the biographies that he jaywalked his way through life before then. Or Bertrand Russell, who as he got older, took greater risks in writing about philosophy, or Mel Torme, who keeps singing publicly at the age of 70 and keeps cresting, never coasting. All of these people never stop. They keep going on, and I began thinking there were other things they had in common.

First, they never thought about past accomplishments, or they didn't think about retiring. In fact, wouldn't a better word be "transitioning" because we're all in transition, and for me, power is the capacity to move from position A to position B, to go on to something else. So these people were always in transition. They were always redesigning, recomposing and reinventing their own lives.

Think about Colin Powell. He was a Second Lieutenant at the Fulda Gap in Germany, a recent graduate of R.O.T.C. Thirty years later he was the commanding general of the whole American Army, and then from there he went to the National

Security Council. Now he's an author, and who knows what he'll be doing next, but you can bet we'll be hearing a lot more about him. Never looking back, never thinking too much about past accomplishments, but always redesigning, recomposing, and reinventing.

What interests me more about all these people, and the successful executives I've known, is that at some point in their lives they stopped trying to prove themselves and began to express themselves. That transition is a very interesting one, one I'm not sure I've accomplished myself. It seems to me there is a profound difference between having to prove yourself versus using the capacity to express yourself.

Bill Bradley, the senator from New Jersey, is a good example of that, because it wasn't until he was almost defeated by Christine Todd Whitman in '92 that he began to think about what he was doing in politics. He began to realize that he was beginning to shade his speeches ever so subtly to please his particular audience. It wasn't that he lied. He just found ways to spin his remarks so that they would please; to seek approval without expressing himself, only trying to prove himself. He said it reminded him of when he played basketball at Princeton, where he was a major college star.

He said, "Even then, when I was playing for the fans, I wasn't nearly as effective a player as when I was playing to do the best I could for the team."

In his last years with the Knicks, Bradley didn't start. He was on the bench. When he left the Knicks, he said, "Those last two years were like participating in my own death." Bradley is a very thoughtful man, someone who gave me the inspiration to think about expressing myself versus proving myself.

**2.** The second general idea I want to argue is that people who have been successful in their careers and in life are also successful in all transitions. I think people who have not been very successful in their lives, in their careers, don't adjust well to any transition. And to them and to me, it's simply death on the installment plan.

As a matter of fact, it made me think about my studies on outstanding leaders. I realized that all of the five characteristics these 150 leaders manifested in their work would be true of successful transitions, or if you will, to use a word that I objected to earlier, successful "retirement." I'm just going to give you a brief summary of the five characteristics.

The first is a strong sense of *purpose,* a passion, a conviction, a sense of wanting to do something important to make a difference. That was true of every single leader. I remember talking with Michael Eisner about his own purposes. He said:

> *I don't know if I have a purpose, but I have a strong point of view. It's also interesting for me to watch my staff at meetings every Friday to see which of the people in that group usually win the day. We make major decisions, hundreds of millions of dollars in new projects and new movies. It's always the person with a strong P.O.V. (as he called it, a strong point of view) that wins the day, that wins the argument. Maybe it's just Hollywood, I don't know, but I'll tell you around here a strong P.O.V. is worth at least 80 I.Q. points.*

Jack Welch, whenever he takes a new job for General Electric, said, "I always want to revolutionize the place." Again, a strong sense of purpose.

Max DePree, the recently retired chairman of Herman Miller, talked about the vision of the company as a spiritual project. (I'm using some examples from my own research on leaders because I think these characteristics make for effective transitioning in the future.) When Max DePree used the phrase "spiritual projects," I recalled that Ernest Becker in his treatise on death talked about the fact that our purposes in life, spiritual projects if you will, are a way in our lifetime of transcending death.

The second thing about these executives is that they were capable of developing and sustaining deep and trusting *relationships.* They seemed to be constant, caring and authentic with other people. If you just take purposes in life and strong intimate human relationships, I think we have at least two of the major secrets of successful transitioning.

The third characteristic is that every single one of the leaders were purveyors of *hope.* It was interesting to me that they all had positive illusions about reality. I had been brought up to think that mental health was dependent on perceiving reality. Now I believe these successful leaders had an almost unreal sense of "We can do it"; "I can do it." The first person I actually studied in depth was in Los Angeles. Shortly after I got to know him, he was diagnosed as having an inoperable brain tumor. He was given three years to live. Well, he just retired, fifteen years after the diagnosis. Through his incredible sense of optimism and hope, this man outlived all the guesses on the median age of people with that condition. As a matter of fact, he wrote a marvelous little essay, a takeoff on McCluhan, called "The Median Ain't the Message."

The fourth point is that all these individuals seemed to have a *balance* in their lives between work, power, and family or outside activities. They didn't tie up all of their self-esteem on their position in the organization. I think that's a danger sign. My predecessor at the University of Cincinnati was there for twenty years. During the student riots, when a rock came through a window in the Administration building, it was as if his skin was broken. It was a personal attack on him. Retirement wasn't easy for him because a year or so after he retired, he died.

I got a letter from a friend of mind recently, who had retired from the *Washington Post,* which stated that he hadn't heard from me after he had written to me. He said, "If I was still with the *Washington Post,* would you have not responded to my letter?" And then he went on to say, "You know I identified myself so much with that newspaper, so much that I used to think that J.E. (his initials) equaled W.P. (JE=WP) and now I feel shorn of my identity." So I think that balance has to be maintained.

Fifth, all of these individuals had a bias toward *action.* They all were people who seemed not to hesitate in taking risks, who while not reckless, were able to take action. They loved adventure, risk and promise.

As an example, I love to reflect on the autobiography of J. Paul Getty. He once wrote that he had three rules for success in business. One was get up early. The second was work hard, and the third was find oil.

I conclude along these lines with a quotation from my favorite management philosopher, the great one, Wayne Gretzky, who said, "You miss 100 percent of the shots you don't take." I think that's what I'm talking about when I talk about successful transitioning.

# INDEX

# ABOUT THE AUTHOR

Warren Bennis is Distinguished Professor of Business Administration and Founding Chairman of The Leadership Institute at the University of Southern California. He has been observing and writing about leaders and managers for more than four decades. His many books include the best-selling *Leaders* and *On Becoming a Leader*, and the Pulitzer Prize-nominated *An Invented Life*.

Bennis has served on the faculties of MIT's Sloan School of Management, Harvard University, and Boston University, and he has been executive vice president of the State University of New York at Buffalo and president of the University of Cincinnati.

He lives in Santa Monica, California.

# Executive **Excellence**

Since 1984, *Executive Excellence* has provided business leaders and managers with the best and latest thinking on leadership development, managerial effectiveness, and organizational productivity. Each issue is filled with insights and answers from top business executives, trainers, and consultants—information you won't find in any other publication.

---

*"Excellent! This is one of the finest newsletters I've seen in the field."*

—Tom Peters, co-author of *In Search of Excellence*

"Executive Excellence *is the* Harvard Business Review *in* USA Today *format."*

—Stephen R. Covey, author of *The 7 Habits of Highly Effective People*

*"Executive Excellence is the best executive advisory newsletter anywhere in the world—it's just a matter of time before a lot more people find that out."*

—Ken Blanchard, co-author of *The One-Minute Manager*

---

**CONTRIBUTING EDITORS INCLUDE**

Stephen R. Covey

Ken Blanchard

Marjorie Blanchard

Charles Garfield

Peter Senge

Gifford Pinchot

Elizabeth Pinchot

**Warren Bennis**

---

**For more information** about *Executive Excellence* or our new publication, *Personal Excellence*, or for information regarding books, audio tapes, CD-ROM, custom editions, reprints, and other products,

please call Executive Excellence Publishing at: **1-800-304-9782**
or visit our web site: **http://www.eep.com**